Essential Tropical Fish
Species Guide

Anne Finlay

Essential Tropical Fish: Species Guide

Copyright © 2023 Elluminet Press

This work is subject to copyright. All rights are reserved by the Publisher, whether the whole or part of the material is concerned, specifically the rights of translation, reprinting, reuse of illustrations, recitation, broadcasting, reproduction on microfilms or in any other physical way, and transmission or information storage and retrieval, electronic adaptation, computer software, or by similar or dissimilar methodology now known or hereafter developed. Exempted from this legal reservation are brief excerpts in connection with reviews or scholarly analysis or material supplied specifically for the purpose of being entered and executed on a computer system, for exclusive use by the purchaser of the work. Duplication of this publication or parts thereof is permitted only under the provisions of the Copyright Law of the Publisher's location, in its current version, and permission for use must always be obtained from the Publisher. Permissions for use may be obtained through Rights Link at the Copyright Clearance Centre. Violations are liable to prosecution under the respective Copyright Law.

Trademarked names, logos, and images may appear in this book. Rather than use a trademark symbol with every occurrence of a trademarked name, logo, or image we use the names, logos, and images only in an editorial fashion and to the benefit of the trademark owner, with no intention of infringement of the trademark.

The use in this publication of trade names, trademarks, service marks, and similar terms, even if they are not identified as such, is not to be taken as an expression of opinion as to whether or not they are subject to proprietary rights.

Fish Images used with permission under CCASA / CC-BY-SA-3.0, Tafkira2, Photo by icon0com form PxHere, ID103189353© Mirkorosenau Dreamstime.com, dianakuehn30010, aquaportail.com, royalty free license from Megapixl.com & Luminescent Media.

While the advice and information in this book are believed to be true and accurate at the date of publication, neither the authors nor the editors nor the publisher can accept any legal responsibility for any errors or omissions that may be made. The publisher makes no warranty, express or implied, with respect to the material contained herein.

Publisher: Elluminet Press
Director: Kevin Wilson
Lead Editor: Mike Smith
Copy Editors: Joanne Taylor
Proof Reader: Robert Price
Indexer: James Marsh
Cover Designer: Kevin Wilson

Table of Contents

About the Author 7
Acknowledgements 9
Introduction 10
    Temperament 11
    Care Difficulty 11
    Water Parameters 12
        Temperature *12*
        Water Hardness *13*
        pH *13*
        Ammonia, Nitrite, and Nitrate Levels *15*
Live-bearers 16
    Platy 17
    Guppy 18
    Endler's Livebearer 19
    Molly 20
    Sword Tail 21
Loaches 22
    Bengal Loach 23
    Big Blue Botia 24
    Burmese Polkadot Loach 25
    Clown Loach 26
    Dwarf Chain Loach 27
    Horse-face Loach 28
    Kuhli Loach 29
    Skunk Loach 30
    Yoyo Loach 31
    Zebra Loach 32
    Weather Loach 33
Cory Catfish 34
    Banded Corydoras 35
    Blackstripe Bondi Corydoras 36
    Blue Corydoras 37
    Bronze Corydoras 38
    Dwarf Corydoras 39
    Hognosed Brochis 40
    Emerald Cory 41
    Elegant Corydoras 42

    Julii Corydoras 43
    Bandit Corydoras 44
    Panda Corydoras 45
    Peppered Corydoras 46
    Salt & Pepper Corydoras 47
    Schwartz's Catfish 48
    Sixray Corydoras 49
    Sterba's Corydoras 50
    Albino Corydoras 51

Plecos **52**
    Bristlenose Pleco 53
    Common Pleco 54
    Gold Nugget Pleco 55
    Leopard Sailfin Pleco 56
    Zebra Pleco 57
    Albino Sailfin Pleco 58
    Royal Pleco 59
    Blue Phantom Pleco 60
    Clown Pleco 61

Other Catfish **62**
    Otocinclus Catfish 63
    Panda Garra 64
    Pictus Catfish 65
    Whiptail Catfish 66
    Featherfin Catfish 67
    Striped Raphael 68
    Banjo Catfish 69

Characins **70**
    Black Phantom Tetra 71
    Black Neon Tetra 72
    Bleeding Heart Tetra 73
    Blood-fin Tetra 74
    Buenos Aires Tetra 75
    Congo Tetra 76
    Emperor Tetra 77
    Glowlight Tetra 78
    Golden Pristella Tetra 79
    Lemon Tetra 80
    Neon Tetra 81
    Penguin Tetra 82
    Red-eye Tetra 83
    Red Phantom Tetra 84

    Rummy Nose Tetra 85
    Serpae Tetra 86
    Silver Dollar 87

Labyrinth Fish **88**
    Chocolate Gourami 89
    Dwarf Gourami 90
    Giant Gourami 91
    Paradise Fish 92
    Pearl Gourami 93
    Three Spot Gourami 94
    Golden Gourami 95
    Pygmy Sparkling Gourami 96
    Silver/Moonlight Gourami 97
    Kissing Gourami 98
    Siamese "Betta" Fighting Fish 99

Cyprinids **100**
    Black Ruby Barb 101
    Checker Barb 102
    Cherry Barb 103
    Clown Barb 104
    Golden Barb 106
    Odessa Barb & One-spot Barb 107
    Red Line Torpedo Barb 108
    Tiger Barb 109
    Tinfoil Barb 110
    Bala Shark 111
    Red-Tailed Black Shark 112
    Ruby Rainbow Shark 113
    Siamese Algae Eater 114
    Harlequin Rasbora 115

Danios **116**
    Giant Danio 117
    Pearl Danio 118
    Glowlight Danio 119
    Zebra Danio 120
    Glofish Danio 121

Angels & Cichlids **122**
    Altum Angelfish 123
    Koi Angelfish 124
    Gold Angelfish 125
    Green Terror Cichlid 126

    Oscar 127
    Rams 128
    Convict Cichlid 129
    Jack Dempsey Cichlid 130
    Bumblebee Cichlid 131
    Blue Dolphin Cichlid 132
    Kribensis Cichlid 133

Discus 134
    Common Discus 135
    Royal Red Discus 136
    Red Checkerboard Discus 137

Rainbow Fish 138
    Red Rainbowfish 139
    Neon Rainbowfish 141

Neotropical Electric Fish 142
    Black Ghost Knifefish 143
    Zebra Knifefish 144
    Elephant Nose 145

Gobies 146
    Bumblebee Goby 147
    Knight Goby 148
    Blue Neon Goby 149

Miscellaneous Fish 150
    Common Hatchet Fish 151
    Three-lined Pencil Fish 152
    Butterfly Fish 153
    Panchax Killifish 154
    Parrot Cichlid 155

Index 156

About the Author

Anne Finlay has had a life long fascination with tropical fish from an early age, starting off with keeping gold fish then moving on to tropical and marine fish.

This led to studying them further at college and working at a public aquarium maintaining the tanks and advising people on the various species.

Her experience of the hobby and the fish trade keeps her abreast of the latest developments and has become the basis for writing this book.

Fish are fascinating to watch and hope you enjoy them as much as we have.

Acknowledgements

Thanks to all the staff at Luminescent Media & Elluminet Press for their passion, dedication and hard work in the preparation and production of this book.

To all my friends and family for their continued support and encouragement in all my writing projects.

1 Introduction

Tropical freshwater fish are a popular choice for aquarium enthusiasts due to their vibrant colors, unique markings, and diverse behaviors. These fish come from various regions of the world where the water is warm and relatively stable in temperature.

One of the most striking features of freshwater tropical fish is their wide range of colors and patterns. From vivid blues, reds, and yellows to subtle pastels and intricate markings, these fish come in a stunning array of hues.

Different species exhibit fascinating behaviors from spectacular schooling displays to territorial and courtship rituals. These behaviors add life and dynamism to the aquarium.

This book contains the most common species found in most aquatic stores and is by no means exhaustive.

First things to take into consideration are the fish's adult size, its temperament, compatibility with other tank-mates, and care difficulty. These are indicated in the book.

Chapter 1: Introduction

Temperament

Peaceful: Species in this category are generally non-threatening and have a calm and passive nature. They prefer peaceful coexistence with tank mates and are unlikely to show aggression. Peaceful fish are usually well-suited for community aquariums, as they rarely engage in territorial disputes. Some peaceful species may exhibit reclusive behaviors, seeking hiding spots among decorations or plants..

Semi-Aggressive: Fish in this category are more active and may occasionally display chasing or aggression, especially towards fish with similar shapes or colors. While they can coexist with other tank mates, it is essential to monitor their behavior to prevent potential conflicts. When introducing semi-aggressive species, do so after establishing smaller, more passive fish in the aquarium. Providing ample space and hiding spots can help reduce aggression among semi-aggressive fish.

Aggressive: Species in this category are territorial and bold. They often establish their territories and may defend them vigorously. Aggressive fish should generally be housed with fish that share a similar demeanor and can stand their ground. Keeping them in a species-only aquarium is recommended, as they might not tolerate other fish well. If adding aggressive fish to a display with semi-aggressive tank mates, they should be the last fish introduced to the tank to minimize territorial disputes.

Care Difficulty

Easy: Fish in this category are undemanding and relatively low-maintenance. They have simple feeding requirements and can tolerate a broad range of water conditions. Easy-care fish are ideal for beginners and can adapt well to various environments. Some examples of easy-care fish include popular community fish like guppies, platies, and neon tetras.

Moderate: Fish in this category require a bit more care and attention to thrive. They might have specific feeding preferences, such as preferring live or frozen foods over standard flakes or pellets. Moderate-care fish may also need water conditions that closely resemble those found in their natural habitat, including specific temperature ranges and water chemistry. Providing suitable tank decorations, plants, and hiding spots can create a more comfortable environment for them. Some examples of moderately demanding fish include certain cichlids, rasboras, and dwarf gouramis.

Chapter 1: Introduction

Difficult: Fish in this category demand a higher level of care and attention, particularly regarding water quality and stability. Many of these species have specific feeding, water, and lighting requirements to maintain their health and vibrant colors. Difficult-care fish should only be added to a well-established aquarium that has been running smoothly for several months. Their tank should be equipped with efficient filtration and regular water testing to ensure pristine water conditions. Examples of difficult-care fish include delicate species like discus, some species of angelfish, and certain types of catfish.

Water Parameters

One of the most critical factors in maintaining the health and well-being of your fish is to ensure that their aquarium water meets their specific requirements. Different fish species have varying preferences when it comes to water conditions, including temperature, pH level, hardness, and other factors. Therefore, it is essential to be aware of and maintain the correct water parameters for the species you are interested in keeping. We have included some general water parameters for each species covered in this book. You can test these parameters using a test kit, which is readily available in most pet stores that stock fish. While most aquarium species can tolerate a broad range of water conditions, keep in mind that certain delicate species of fish have very specific water parameter requirements. If you are using tap water, then you will need a water conditioner.

Temperature

Temperature plays a crucial role in the overall health and behavior of fish. Many tropical fish species thrive in water temperatures ranging from 75°F to 82°F (24°C to 28°C). However, some species might prefer cooler or warmer conditions. For instance, coldwater fish such as goldfish and certain species of tetras prefer lower temperatures around 68°F to 74°F (20°C to 23°C). Use a reliable aquarium thermometer to monitor and maintain a consistent temperature suitable for the specific fish you have..

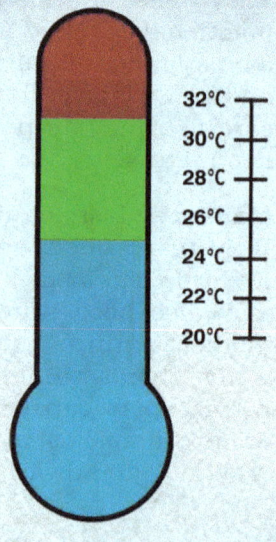

Fish are cold blooded and are very sensitive to temperature changes and any sudden temperature change can wreak havoc on your fish. Invest in a reliable heater to maintain a stable water temperature.

Chapter 1: Introduction

Water Hardness

Water hardness refers to the concentration of minerals, primarily calcium and magnesium, in your aquarium water. Understanding the two main aspects of water hardness is essential for maintaining a healthy aquatic environment:

Carbonate hardness (KH), often referred to as KH, measures the concentration of carbonate and bicarbonate ions in the water. KH acts as the main buffering capacity of the water, helping it resist drastic changes in pH levels. When the KH is high, the pH tends to remain stable, which is beneficial for the overall health of fish and other aquatic organisms. A dKH between 4 and 12 is recommended.

dKH	Tank
4-8 dKH	Tropical Fish
10-18 dKH	African Cichlid
3-8 dKH	Discus
10-18 dKH	Brackish
3-8 dKH	Planted

General hardness (GH), often referred to as GH, measures the concentration of calcium and magnesium ions in the water. Different aquatic species have specific preferences for water hardness. Some thrive in "hard" water, which contains a higher mineral content, while others prefer "soft" water, with lower mineral levels. GH is typically measured in degrees of hardness (dH), where higher values indicate harder water and lower values indicate softer water.

°Degrees of Hardness	Description
0-6	Soft Water
6-12	Moderately Hard
12-20	Hard Water
20-30	Very Hard Water

Both KH and GH levels are usually measured in dKH or dGH (degrees of hardness), with 1 dKH or dGH equivalent to 17.9 ppm (parts per million) of the respective mineral. Purchase a water hardness test kit from a pet store or online retailer.

pH

The pH level of your aquarium water indicates its acidity or alkalinity. Most tropical fish prefer a pH range between 6.5 to 7.5, which is slightly acidic to neutral.

The pH level directly impacts the health, behavior, and overall well-being of the fish. Different species have specific pH preferences based on their natural habitats. Therefore, maintaining the appropriate pH range is crucial to support their biological processes and reduce stress.

Chapter 1: Introduction

Regularly test the pH level and make adjustments if needed to meet the preferences of your fish. The pH is the measurement of relative alkalinity or acidity of the water.

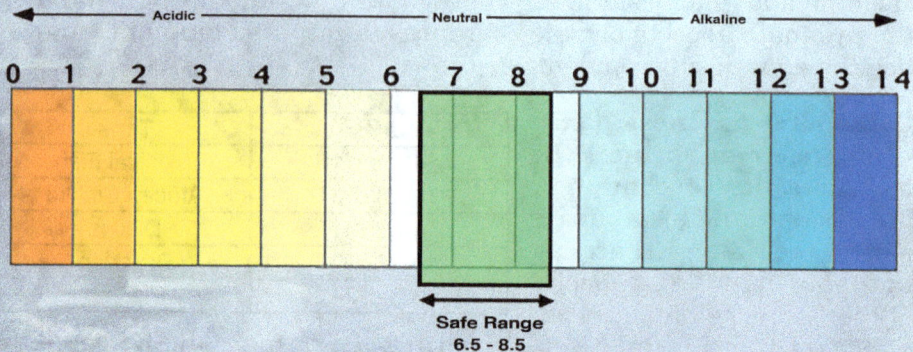

A pH reading of 7.0 is considered neutral.

Lower than 7.0 (down to 0) is acidic.

Higher than 7.0 (up to 14) is alkaline.

Some factors can affect the pH of your aquarium. The pH of your tap water may vary depending on your location and the water source. Some areas have naturally alkaline water, while others may have more acidic water.

The nitrogen cycle, which involves the conversion of ammonia to nitrite and then nitrate, can influence pH levels in the aquarium. Ammonia can make the water more acidic, while nitrates can make it slightly more alkaline.

Some substrates, such as crushed coral or limestone, can increase the pH and hardness of the water, making it more alkaline. On the other hand, driftwood or peat moss can have an acidic effect on the water.

To control pH levels in your aquarium, you can use various methods:

- **Buffering Substances:** Adding commercial pH buffers can help stabilize pH levels and prevent rapid fluctuations.

- **Driftwood and Peat Moss:** If your water is too alkaline, adding driftwood or peat moss can help lower the pH.

- **Crushed coral or limestone:** If your water is too acidic, adding crushed coral or limestone can help raise the pH.

- **Aeration:** Proper aeration can help maintain a stable pH level by releasing excess CO_2.

Chapter 1: Introduction

Ammonia, Nitrite, and Nitrate Levels

Regularly monitor ammonia, nitrite, and nitrate levels in your aquarium. Ammonia and nitrite are harmful to fish, and high levels can lead to stress and even death. A well-established aquarium should have undetectable ammonia and nitrite levels. Nitrate is a byproduct of the nitrogen cycle and should be kept at low levels (less than 20 ppm). Perform regular water changes to control these parameters and maintain a healthy nitrogen cycle.

For your tank to be successful, you need to establish the nitrogen cycle.

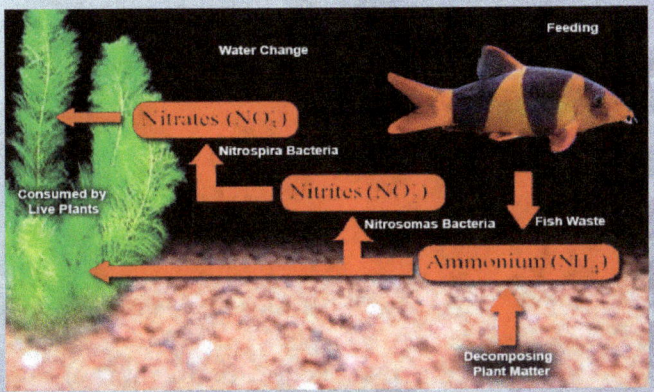

The nitrogen cycle begins with the release of ammonia (NH_3) into the water. Ammonia is produced mainly from fish waste, uneaten food, and decaying organic matter. Ammonia is highly toxic and can cause stress, illness, and death if present in high concentrations.

Ammonia is converted into nitrite (NO_2^-) through a process called nitrification. This is accomplished by a group of bacteria called Nitrosomonas. These beneficial bacteria oxidize ammonia, transforming it into nitrite, which is also harmful to fish in high concentrations.

Nitrite (NO_2^-) is further converted into nitrate (NO_3^-) by another group of beneficial bacteria called Nitrobacter. This process is known as the second stage of nitrification. Nitrate is less toxic to fish and can be tolerated at low to moderate levels.

Nitrate (NO_3^-) is the final product of the nitrogen cycle. While it is less toxic than ammonia and nitrite, excessive nitrate levels can still be harmful to fish and other aquatic life, especially at high concentrations. In a well-maintained aquarium, nitrate levels should be regularly reduced through water changes and by the uptake of nitrates by live plants.

2 Live-bearers

As the name suggests, these fish give birth to live young instead of laying eggs.

Poeciliidae, commonly known as livebearers, are all very hardy and are considered to be a good fish for beginners, are a lot of fun and many experienced fish keepers continue to delight in keeping them!

Because these fish bare live young, they can breed quite rapidly. So keep this in mind if you mix males and females. It is recommended that males and females are not mixed as they will breed and males will relentlessly hassle females.

There are lots of different varieties with lots of different colours readily available.

They tend to inhabit the top and middle of the aquarium but go down to the bottom now and again.

Chapter 2: Livebearers

Platy

Distinct in their vibrant hues and assorted patterns, platies showcase a spectrum of colors including red, black, blue, and combinations like the tuxedo - a fusion of red and black. Despite this variation in coloration, they remain consistent in terms of their general shape and size.

Scientific Name: Xiphophorus maculatus
Care Level: Beginner-friendly
Temperament: Peaceful and sociable
Maximum Size: Up to 3 inches (approximately 7.5 cm)
Minimum Tank Size: Requires at least a 10-gallon (40-liter) tank
Water Conditions: Prefers temperatures between 64-78° F (17-25° C), dH 5-20, and pH 7.0-8.2
Diet: Omnivorous; thrives on a balanced diet of quality flake food
Origin: Native to North and Central America
Aquarium Type: Suitable for community aquarium setups

Notes
Platies appreciate a well-planted aquarium, favoring hardy plant species like java fern and java moss.
Their peaceful nature makes them compatible with other non-aggressive fish, and they flourish best when kept in small groups of at least three.
Although omnivorous, platies thrive on a varied diet comprising prepared flake and algae-based foods. Remember to avoid housing them with aggressive species for the best results.

Chapter 2: Livebearers

Guppy

With their kaleidoscope of colors, guppies are a sight to behold when kept in groups of six or more. While the males bear a more vibrant color palette, females exhibit larger physical dimensions, adding to the aesthetic diversity of these tropical fish.

Scientific Name: Poecilia reticulata
Care Level: Beginner-friendly
Temperament: Peaceful and social
Maximum Size: Up to 2 inches (around 5 cm)
Minimum Tank Size: Requires at least a 10-gallon (40-liter) tank
Water Conditions: Prefers temperatures between 64-82° F (17-27° C), dH 10-30, and pH 7-8.4
Diet: Omnivorous; thrives on quality flake food and a varied diet
Origin: Indigenous to South America and the Caribbean
Aquarium Type: Well-suited for community aquarium setups

Notes:
Guppies are renowned for their hardiness and playful nature, making them excellent choices for those new to fishkeeping. They flourish in well-planted tanks, where they have ample space to swim freely. Given their rapid breeding capacity, care should be exercised when housing males and females together, with a preference for all-male tanks to prevent overpopulation. Guppies benefit from a balanced diet that includes both plant-based and meaty foods. An algae-based flake food complemented by freeze-dried bloodworms, tubifex, and brine shrimp ensures their nutritional needs are adequately met. Despite their peaceful temperament, guppies should be kept away from fin-nipping species like barbs and tetras, as these could harm the guppies' prominent tail fins.

Chapter 2: Livebearers

Endler's Livebearer

Endler's Livebearers bear a striking resemblance to their guppy cousins, albeit with smaller stature. These fish dazzle in large shoals of around 12 or more, with varying markings that add to their allure while generally retaining a consistent shape and size.

Scientific Name: Poecilia wingei
Care Level: Beginner-friendly
Temperament: Peaceful and sociable
Maximum Size: Up to 1 inch (approximately 2.5 cm)
Minimum Tank Size: At least a 20-gallon (75-liter) tank is recommended
Water Conditions: Prefers temperatures between 64-82° F (17-25° C), dH 10-20, and pH 6.5-8.0
Diet: Omnivorous, requires a balanced diet
Origin: Native to Venezuela
Aquarium Type: Ideal for community aquarium setups

Notes:
Endler's Livebearers thrive in groups of at least six, but be wary of housing them with known fin-nippers like barbs or tetras, as these could damage the delicate tail fins of these livebearers. Hardy plant varieties such as java fern and java moss are recommended for their tank, given their ability to handle increased hardness in the aquarium. Other peaceful fish species would make excellent tank mates for Endler's Livebearers. As omnivores, they require a well-rounded diet consisting of both plant-based and meaty foods. An algae-based flake food, complemented by occasional protein sources, would be sufficient to meet their nutritional needs.

Chapter 2: Livebearers

Molly

Known for their vivacious and alert nature, mollies can be conditioned to recognize their keepers, eagerly swimming up to the glass or even accepting food directly from your hand with a bit of patience. Despite varying markings, they generally maintain a similar shape and size.

Scientific Name: Poecilia latipinna
Care Level: Beginner-friendly
Temperament: Peaceful and sociable
Maximum Size: Can grow up to 4-5 inches (around 10 cm)
Minimum Tank Size: Requires at least a 20-gallon (75-liter) tank
Water Conditions: Prefers temperatures between 75-82° F (23-27° C), dH 10-25, and pH 7.5-8.5
Diet: Omnivorous; thrives on quality flake food and a balanced diet
Origin: Indigenous to Central America
Aquarium Type: Well-suited for community aquarium setups

Notes:
Mollies flourish in at least a 20-gallon tank that's densely populated with sturdy plants like java fern, sagittaria, vallisneria, and anubias. Owing to their hearty appetites, they require a robust filtration system to maintain water quality. They are not fussy eaters and will readily consume an algae-based flake food, as well as freeze-dried bloodworms, tubifex, and brine shrimp, which they particularly enjoy. While mollies are peaceful and compatible with most other non-aggressive species, it's advisable to keep them in groups of at least three to promote their social behavior.

Chapter 2: Livebearers

Sword Tail

Swordtails are easily identifiable by their unique, sword-like tail fin. They showcase an array of markings and colours, while their overall shape and size remain generally consistent.

Scientific Name: Xiphophorus hellerii
Care Level: Easy, ideal for beginners
Temperament: Peaceful, sociable species
Maximum Size: Can reach up to 4 inches (around 10 cm)
Minimum Tank Size: Needs at least a 20-gallon (75-liter) tank
Water Conditions: Prefers temperatures between 64-82° F (17-25° C), dH 12-30, and pH 7.0-8.3
Diet: Omnivorous; thrives on a diet of quality flake food
Origin: Native to Central America and China
Aquarium Type: Well-suited for community aquarium setups

Notes:
These guys require an aquarium of at least 20 gallons that is well planted with plenty of room for swimming. Also provide plenty of shelter. Swordtails are omnivore and will eat flaked foods as well as freeze dried bloodworms, tubifex and brine shrimp. Swordtails seem to be compatible with most other peaceful fish and are best kept in groups of 3 or more. While Swordtails are generally peaceful, males can sometimes display aggression towards each other, particularly in a crowded space or when females are present. Therefore, maintaining a balanced gender ratio can be beneficial to reduce potential aggression.

3 Loaches

As active scavengers residing predominantly at the bottom of their habitats, loaches — part of the Cobitidae family — are perfectly suited for community aquariums. These vibrant and intriguing creatures are amongst the most sought-after tropical fish, enhancing the aesthetic appeal and dynamism of any sizable community aquarium with their lively presence.

However, it's crucial to remember that some loach species can grow considerably large. This growth potential should be taken into account when considering adding loaches to your aquarium, as they will require ample space to move around.

Social by nature, loaches thrive best in the company of their own kind. They should be kept in groups of six or more to foster a harmonious environment and minimize potential aggression. It is not advisable to keep a loach in solitude, as this can lead to stress and disruptive behavior.

Chapter 3: Loaches

Bengal Loach

Recognizable for their distinct patterns of stripes and spots, Bengal Loaches, also known as Geto or Queen Loaches, add an exotic appeal to any aquarium.

Scientific Name: Botia dario
Care Level: Easy, suitable for beginners and experienced aquarists
Temperament: Generally peaceful; a bottom dweller by nature
Maximum Size: Can grow up to 6 inches (around 15 cm)
Minimum Tank Size: Requires at least a 70-gallon (250-liter) aquarium
Water Conditions: Prefers temperatures between 72-86° F (22-30° C), dH 8-12, and pH 6.0-7.5
Diet: Carnivorous; thrives on a diet of high-quality sinking pellet food
Origin: Native to Bangladesh and India
Aquarium Type: An excellent addition to community tanks

Notes:
Bengal Loaches are social creatures and should ideally be kept in groups of at least five to ensure their well-being. While they are generally peaceful towards other fish species, there have been instances of some individuals showing signs of aggression, primarily directed at their own kind. They are generally compatible with most other species, except those with long fins, which might provoke them. For their comfort, the tank substrate should be comprised of fine sand, as this protects their sensitive barbels, and the aquarium should provide plenty of hiding spots such as rocky caves and robust aquatic plants. Subdued lighting is also preferable to mimic their natural habitat conditions.

Chapter 3: Loaches

Big Blue Botia

Sharing a striking resemblance with Clown Loaches, the Big Blue Botia stand out due to their heightened aggression towards each other.

Scientific Name: Yasuhikotakia modesta
Care Level: Moderate; requires more attention due to its territorial nature
Temperament: Can be highly territorial, and in-fighting is common
Maximum Size: Can grow up to 10-12 inches (about 30 cm)
Minimum Tank Size: Requires at least a 75-gallon (300-liter) aquarium
Water Conditions: Prefers temperatures between 78-86° F (25-30° C), dH 8-12, and pH 6.0-7.5
Diet: Omnivorous; thrives on a diet of high-quality flake food, sinking pellets, algae wafers, and fresh vegetables like cucumber
Origin: Native to Cambodia
Aquarium Type: Ideally suited for larger community tanks; resides at the bottom

Notes:
Due to their social nature, Big Blue Botias should be kept in groups of at least five. They get along well with other peaceful species like Rasboras, Barbs, Corydoras, Danios, Catfish, and other robust Loaches.

Ensure their environment includes ample cover, caves, hiding spots, and plants. The tank substrate should be fine to mimic their natural habitat and protect their delicate underbelly. These provisions will help minimize stress and territorial disputes while promoting a sense of safety and security.

Chapter 3: Loaches

Burmese Polkadot Loach

Resembling their relatives, the Bengal Loaches, the Burmese Polkadot Loaches distinguish themselves with their distinctive spotted appearance.

Scientific Name: Botia kubotai
Care Level: Moderate, requiring a little extra attention
Temperament: Generally peaceful and dwell near the bottom of the tank
Maximum Size: Can grow up to 4-5 inches (approximately 12 cm)
Minimum Tank Size: Requires at least a 50-gallon (200-liter) aquarium
Water Conditions: Prefers temperatures between 72-86° F (23-30° C), dH 8-12, and pH 6.0-7.5
Diet: Omnivorous; prefers high-quality sinking pellet food and enjoys fresh produce like cucumber
Origin: Native to India
Aquarium Type: Suited for a community tank

Notes:
Burmese Polkadot Loaches favor a naturally styled aquarium with fine substrate, adorned with stones, driftwood roots, or branches. The presence of live plants, rocks, and terra cotta pots providing plenty of hiding spots is crucial for their well-being. A socially inclined species, these loaches thrive in groups of five or more. Compatibility with most other peaceful fish species makes them a versatile addition to a community tank. However, remember to keep a close eye on them to ensure a harmonious environment. These loaches seem compatible with most other peaceful fish.

Chapter 3: Loaches

Clown Loach

Clown Loaches, distinguished by their vibrant black and gold stripes and radiant scarlet fins, are a delightful and animated addition to any tank. They are notable for their playful and entertaining behavior.

Scientific Name: Chromobotia macracanthus
Care Level: Moderate, requiring consistent monitoring
Temperament: Generally peaceful
Maximum Size: Can grow up to 12 inches (approximately 30 cm)
Minimum Tank Size: Requires at least a 75-80-gallon (300-liter) aquarium
Water Conditions: Prefers temperatures between 76-86° F (25-30° C), dH 8-12, and pH 6.0-7.5
Diet: Omnivorous; they adore cucumbers, are excellent for controlling pest snails, and have a strong appetite for worm-like foods such as frozen bloodworms. A high-quality pellet food also suits them well.
Origin: Native to Indonesia
Aquarium Type: Ideal for a large community tank.

Notes

Clown Loaches thrive in social groups, optimally in batches of 10 to 12, particularly in larger tanks. Their habitat should feature plenty of hiding places, caves, and be well populated with plants. A fine substrate is essential for their comfort. However, keep in mind that they may nibble on delicate plants, so ensure to select hardy varieties when setting up the aquarium. Compatibility with other peaceful species, including livebearers, rasboras, barbs, corydoras, danios, catfish, and other loaches, makes them an adaptable choice for a community tank. Regular monitoring can ensure a harmonious environment for all residents. They also exhibit entertaining, clown-like antics such as lying on their sides or back to sleep, making clicking sounds to communicate, and piling on top of each other in a tight corner or space.

Chapter 3: Loaches

Dwarf Chain Loach

Dwarf Chain Loaches, characterized by their diminutive size and distinctive 'chain-like' arrangement of spots along their sides, bring unique charm to an aquarium.

Scientific Name: Ambastaia sidthimunki
Care Level: Moderate, requiring consistent monitoring
Temperament: Generally peaceful, though can display semi-aggressive tendencies
Maximum Size: Grows up to approximately 2.5 inches (6 cm)
Minimum Tank Size: Requires at least a 30-gallon (120-liter) aquarium
Water Conditions: Thrives in temperatures between 76-86° F (25-30° C), dH 8-12, and pH 6.0-7.5
Diet: Omnivorous; a good quality sinking pellet is recommended. They also enjoy a variety of small foods, such as freeze-dried bloodworms, artemia, daphnia, and occasional fresh cucumber.
Origin: Native to Thailand
Aquarium Type: Suited for a community tank

Notes:
Dwarf Chain Loaches flourish in a well-planted tank environment. They remain relatively small and are best housed in groups of three or more with diffused lighting. Another perk of owning these loaches is their ability to control pest snails, adding to their appeal as community tank residents. Despite their compatibility with most species, they can sometimes exhibit aggressiveness, including nipping at other species. Regular monitoring can help manage these occasional bouts of aggression, ensuring a harmonious environment for all fish.

Chapter 3: Loaches

Horse-face Loach

This fascinating species, known as the Horse-face Loach, can be easily distinguished by its unique horse-like facial structure.

Scientific Name: Acantopsis choirorhynchos
Care Level: Moderate
Temperament: Generally peaceful, but may exhibit territorial behavior
Maximum Size: 8" (20cm)
Minimum Tank Size: 50 Gallon (200 litres)
Water Conditions: 79-86° F (26-30° C), dH 3-5, pH 6.0-6.5
Diet: Omnivore
Origin: Southeast Asia
Aquarium Type: Community

Notes:
The Horse-face Loach is a nocturnal species, so providing areas of dim light or darkness will make these fish feel more secure and comfortable. During the day, they often burrow into the substrate, leaving only their eyes visible. This behavior makes them an exciting addition to a community tank. These loaches are best kept in groups of 5 or more and can be kept with danios, cyprinids, and other loaches. Due to their potentially aggressive or territorial behavior, these fish are best kept with species that tend to swim in the upper levels of the tank. However, when kept in proper conditions and with suitable tank mates, Horse-face Loaches generally exhibit peaceful behavior. Provide them with a diet of high-quality sinking foods supplemented with frozen foods such as bloodworms, artemia, and daphnia. It's important to note that these loaches also enjoy hunting for small live foods, which can make feeding them a more interactive experience. Remember that the substrate in your aquarium should be fine and soft, as Horse-face Loaches enjoy digging and burrowing. Sharp or rough substrate can damage their delicate undersides. Consider a sand substrate or fine, smooth gravel.

Chapter 3: Loaches

Kuhli Loach

The Kuhli Loach, renowned for its elongated, slender form, harbors a fondness for digging. Therefore, it is essential to incorporate a soft sandy substrate in their tank.

Scientific Name: Pangio kuhlii
Care Level: Moderate
Temperament: Peaceful
Maximum Size: 5" (12cm)
Minimum Tank Size: 20 Gallon (75 litre)
Water Conditions: 79-86° F, 25-30° C, dH 3-5, pH 6.0-6.5
Diet: Carnivorous
Origin: Indonesia
Aquarium Type: Community

Notes:
Being predominantly nocturnal, Kuhli Loaches are somewhat reticent creatures, preferring to take refuge among the roots of plants, driftwood, rocks, and cave-like structures within the aquarium. Their placid demeanor allows them to cohabit harmoniously with other non-aggressive fish species. As scavengers with a carnivorous diet, these loaches have a proclivity for freeze-dried bloodworms and tubifex, supplemented with a variety of frozen foodstuffs. Despite their scavenging habits, it is essential to ensure they receive sufficient food, as more active tank mates might outcompete them during feeding times.

Chapter 3: Loaches

Skunk Loach

Recognized alternatively as Hora's Loach, the Skunk Loach is easily distinguishable by its distinctive black markings that run along the top of its body, reminiscent of a skunk's patterning.

Scientific Name: Yasuhikotakia morleti
Care Level: Moderate
Temperament: Generally peaceful, can display sporadic bouts of aggression
Maximum Size: 4" (10cm)
Minimum Tank Size: 30 Gallon (115 litre)
Water Conditions: 75-79° F, 24-26° C, dH 5-12, pH 6.5-7.5
Diet: Omnivorous
Origin: Thailand
Aquarium Type: Community

Notes:
Skunk Loaches ideally thrive in groups of 5 or more. Care should be taken when choosing tank mates; compatible species include rasboras, danios, catfish, and other similarly sized loaches. It is advisable to avoid housing them with slow-moving, long-finned fish due to their tendency to fin nip. The inclusion of a fine substrate is crucial, as these loaches are fond of burrowing underneath rocks. Moreover, incorporating driftwood branches and live plants will provide ample hiding places, aligning with their preference for a complex environment. Their diet should consist of a mixture of frozen foods, complemented by high-quality sinking pellet food to ensure nutritional balance.

Chapter 3: Loaches

Yoyo Loach

Commonly referred to as the Almora or Pakistani Loach, the Yoyo Loach bears a striking resemblance to the Bengal Loach.

Scientific Name: Botia almorhae
Care Level: Easy
Temperament: Generally Peaceful
Maximum Size: 6" (15cm)
Minimum Tank Size: 55 Gallon (210 litre)
Water Conditions: 72-79° F, 22-26° C, dH 8-12, pH 6.5-7.5
Diet: Omnivorous
Origin: India and Nepal
Aquarium Type: Community

Notes:
These loaches thrive best when kept in groups of 5 or more and make great tank mates for small to medium-sized robust species such as certain danios and barbs. To protect their delicate barbels, a fine substrate is recommended. Their habitat should also incorporate numerous hiding places including elements such as bogwood, caves, and aquatic plants. Subdued lighting will further mimic their natural environment. Yoyo Loaches should be fed a diet that includes a good quality sinking pellet. They also enjoy fresh vegetables like cucumber on occasion. A beneficial addition to any tank, these loaches are also known to consume pest snails. Although they are generally peaceful, they can occasionally exhibit semi-aggressive behavior, particularly if they are kept in smaller groups or if the aquarium is too small.

Chapter 3: Loaches

Zebra Loach

Also known as the candy-striped loach, the zebra loach can be readily identified by its black stripes that run down its body, evoking the image of a zebra.

Scientific Name: Botia striata
Care Level: Easy
Temperament: Generally Peaceful
Maximum Size: 4" (10cm)
Minimum Tank Size: 40 Gallons (150 litres)
Optimal Water Conditions: 73-80° F (22-26° C), dH 3-5, pH 6.0-6.5
Diet: Omnivorous
Origin: Western India
Preferred Aquarium Type: Community

Notes:
Zebra loaches thrive when kept in groups of five or more, and they can coexist peacefully with species like rasboras, danios, catfish, and other loaches. They prefer environments with sandy substrate, smooth stones, and pieces of driftwood, roots or branches. Providing numerous hiding spots will ensure their comfort. Feed them a staple diet of high-quality sinking pellet foods supplemented with frozen foods such as bloodworms, daphnia, and artemia. An occasional treat of cucumber can also be given. Moreover, zebra loaches are beneficial for controlling pest snails in the aquarium. Zebra loaches are generally peaceful but can show territorial behaviors if they feel crowded or stressed, so ensure they have ample space.

Chapter 3: Loaches

Weather Loach

Also known as the pond loach, Dojo Loach, or Japanese Weather Loach, this species features a long, slender body and is usually gold/orange or brown/white with grey spots.

Scientific Name: Misgurnus anguillicaudatus
Care Level: Moderate
Temperament: Generally Peaceful
Maximum Size: 10" (25cm)
Minimum Tank Size: 50 Gallons (200 litres)
Optimal Water Conditions: 64-75° F (17-24° C), dH 3-5, pH 6.0-8.0
Diet: Omnivorous
Origin: East Asia
Preferred Aquarium Type: Cold Water Community

Notes:
Weather loaches thrive in cooler temperatures than most tropical fish, thus limiting the range of potential tank mates. They are best suited to cohabitate with other cold-water species such as goldfish. These loaches require ample space to move around freely. A soft, fine substrate is essential as they enjoy digging and burying themselves up to their heads. Coarse gravel or stones should be avoided to prevent injury. Their diet should consist of sinking pellets and a variety of frozen foods, such as bloodworms. Live foods also make an excellent addition to their diet. Given their peaceful nature, weather loaches usually get along well with other species. However, their preference for cooler temperatures needs to be considered when selecting tank mates. Additionally, because these loaches are known to be excellent escape artists, make sure your tank has a secure lid.

Cory Catfish

Corydoras, commonly known as Cory Cats, belong to the Callichthyidae family. They are some of the most peaceful and entertaining scavengers you can add to a freshwater aquarium. Not only do they thrive in a diverse range of water conditions, but they also exhibit engaging social behaviors.

Despite their small size, Cory Cats are incredibly efficient and energetic scavengers. Their natural inclination to sift through the substrate makes them ideal for maintaining cleanliness in a small to mid-sized freshwater community aquarium.

Cory Cats are generally compatible with other peaceful bottom dwellers and similarly sized fish. However, they should not be housed with aggressive species, as their peaceful nature makes them vulnerable to harassment or attacks.

Remember, like many schooling fish, Cory Cats do best in groups of six or more of their own kind. A well-planted tank with plenty of hiding spots and soft substrate to protect their delicate barbels is the ideal setup for these delightful catfish.

Chapter 4: Cory Catfish

Banded Corydoras

Also recognized as the Barbatus Cory, the Banded Corydoras can be distinguished by its distinctive gold and black bands.

Scientific Name: Scleromystax barbatus
Care Level: Moderate
Temperament: Generally peaceful, although males can display territorial behavior
Maximum Size: 5" (12cm)
Minimum Tank Size: 60 Gallon (220 liters)
Water Conditions: 68-75° F, 20-23° C, dH 8-10, pH 6.8-7.2
Diet: Omnivorous; feed them a good quality sinking pellet
Origin: Brazil
Aquarium Type: Community

Notes:
These corydoras thrive in groups of 5 or more and favor a well-planted aquarium with plenty of hiding spots and fine substrate. They generally coexist peacefully with most other non-aggressive species, but it's not advisable to mix them with predatory or aggressive fish. Their diet should consist of dried and frozen foods, supplemented with algae wafers or spirulina to ensure balanced nutrition. As these fish love to dig, sharp or rough substrate can harm them. Smooth sand or small, round gravel is best to protect their sensitive barbels and undersides. Banded Corydoras may show more vibrant colors and be more active in a tank with a darker substrate and subdued lighting.

Chapter 4: Cory Catfish

Blackstripe Bondi Corydoras

This particular species of corydoras can be distinguished by the striking black stripe that traverses the length of its body.

Scientific Name: Corydoras bondi
Care Level: Moderate
Temperament: Generally Peaceful
Maximum Size: 2" (5cm)
Minimum Tank Size: 20 Gallon (75 litre)
Water Conditions: 68-78° F, 20-25° C, dH 2-15, pH 6.0-7.8
Diet: Omnivore with a preference for meaty foods
Origin: South America
Aquarium Type: Community

Notes:
Blackstripe Bondi Corydoras thrive when kept in groups of 6 or more, relishing a well-planted aquarium replete with cover and a fine, soft substrate. They thrive best in soft, slightly acidic to neutral water, and they prefer water that is well-oxygenated with a moderate current. These fish coexist harmoniously with a variety of other peaceful species, including other types of cories. However, it's advisable to avoid housing them with predatory or aggressive fish. Their diet should consist of a balance between sinking algae pellets and flake food, supplemented with other sinking foods such as catfish pellets. They also appreciate occasional servings of live or frozen foods like bloodworms or brine shrimp.

Chapter 4: Cory Catfish

Blue Corydoras

Also known as Natterer's catfish, these Corydoras boast a beautiful blue shade accented by a deep blue stripe.

Scientific Name: Corydoras nattereri
Care Level: Easy
Temperament: Peaceful
Maximum Size: 2" (5cm)
Minimum Tank Size: 20 Gallon (approximately 75 liters)
Water Conditions: 68-78° F (20-25° C), dH 2-15, pH 6.0-7.2
Diet: Omnivore – Feed them a high-quality sinking pellet as staple food
Origin: South America
Aquarium Type: Community

Notes:
Corydoras Nattereri are highly social and prefer being in groups of at least five. A well-planted aquarium with ample hiding spots and a fine substrate is an ideal environment for them. These fish are generally compatible with other peaceful species and Corydoras, but they should not be housed with predatory or overly aggressive fish. In addition to a diet of high-quality sinking pellets, they should also be provided with a variety of other foods, including flake food, frozen or freeze-dried bloodworms, daphnia, and brine shrimp to ensure a balanced diet. Including some vegetable matter, such as boiled peas, is also beneficial. As with all Corydoras, a key point to remember is that they are sensitive to high nitrate levels and poor water quality.

Chapter 4: Cory Catfish

Bronze Corydoras

Also known as the lightspot corydoras or wavy catfish, the Bronze Corydoras is typically a beautiful green-brown colour.

Scientific Name: Corydoras aeneus
Care Level: Easy
Temperament: Peaceful
Maximum Size: 3" (7cm)
Minimum Tank Size: 20 Gallon (75 litre)
Water Conditions: 72-78° F, 22-26° C, dH 2-15, pH 6.0-7.5
Diet: Omnivorous - A well-balanced diet that includes a good quality sinking pellet is recommended
Origin: South America
Aquarium Type: Community

Notes:
The Bronze Corydoras thrive best in groups of at least 5 or more, and are compatible with a variety of other peaceful species such as tetras, barbs, livebearers, cyprinids, and dwarf cichlids. For their habitat, it is best to provide a well-planted tank with ample hiding spaces and a fine substrate that facilitates their digging and foraging behaviour. Their diet should include sinking pellets complemented by a variety of frozen foods such as brine shrimp and bloodworms. Occasionally, they also enjoy blanched vegetables. Lastly, it's crucial to make sure any sharp objects or decorations are not present in the tank, as these can damage the delicate barbels (whiskers) of the Corydoras. These barbels are crucial for their scavenging and exploratory activities on the substrate.

Chapter 4: Cory Catfish

Dwarf Corydoras

The Dwarf Corydoras, also known as the Tail Spot Pygmy Catfish or Micro Catfish, typically displays a white-olive coloration.

Scientific Name: Corydoras hastatus
Care Level: Easy
Temperament: Peaceful
Maximum Size: 1" (2.5cm)
Minimum Tank Size: 10 Gallon (40 litre)
Water Conditions: 72-79° F, 22-26° C, dH 2-15, pH 6.0-7.2
Diet: Omnivore – high-quality micro pellets are recommended
Origin: Amazon River
Aquarium Type: Community

Notes:
These Corydoras are sociable fish and prefer to be kept in groups of at least 5. They cohabitate well with other peaceful, similarly sized species. These diminutive fish prefer a dimly lit, heavily planted tank. It should be adorned with fine substrate, pieces of bogwood and twisted roots, and numerous hiding places. Ensure that all food provided is suitably small for their mouths. They can consume dried foods, but these should be of a small grade or finely ground. A varied diet that includes both plant-based and protein-rich foods will help to maintain their health and color. Unlike most other Corydoras who are bottom dwellers, the Dwarf Corydoras (Corydoras Hastatus) is known to swim in the middle and upper levels of the water column, especially when kept in larger groups. Therefore, when observing the tank for these fish, don't forget to look beyond the tank floor.

Chapter 4: Cory Catfish

Hognosed Brochis

The Hognosed Brochis, also identified by its extended snout and head, usually features green coloring on its sides.

Scientific Name: Brochis multiradiatus
Care Level: Easy
Temperament: Peaceful
Maximum Size: 4" (10cm)
Minimum Tank Size: 40 Gallons (150 litres)
Water Conditions: 68-75° F (20-23° C), dH 8-10, pH 6.8-7.2
Diet: Omnivore
Origin: Amazon River
Aquarium Type: Community

Notes:
The Hognosed Brochis is an excellent addition to the community tank. It thrives with species such as characins, cyprinids, anabantids, dwarf cichlids, and other catfish. It prefers a fine substrate in a well-planted tank with plenty of hiding places. For optimal social interaction, they are best kept in groups of five or more. Feed them a varied diet comprising sinking pellets or wafers, coupled with frozen foods like brine shrimp, tubifex worms, and bloodworms. They also appreciate occasional blanched vegetables. Although they are peaceful, Hognosed Brochis can sometimes be quite lively and exhibit fascinating, playful behavior when they feel secure in their environment. Their longer snout is used to rummage through the substrate for food, so soft sand or smooth gravel would be ideal to prevent any injuries.

Chapter 4: Cory Catfish

Emerald Cory

Recognizable by its emerald green body highlighted with pink undertones on its lower parts and underbelly, the Emerald Corydoras is a captivating addition to any aquarium.

Scientific Name: Corydoras splendens
Care Level: Easy
Temperament: Peaceful
Maximum Size: 3" (7cm)
Minimum Tank Size: 30 Gallons (115 litres)
Water Conditions: 68-75° F (20-23° C), dH 8-10, pH 6.8-7.2
Diet: Omnivorous
Origin: South America
Aquarium Type: Community

Notes:
Emerald Corydoras thrive in community tanks and exhibit compatibility with characins, cyprinids, anabantids, dwarf cichlids, and other catfish. A well-planted aquarium, teeming with hiding spots and fine substrate, suits them best. It's recommended to keep these sociable fish in groups of at least five. A varied diet is key to their health. Feed them sinking pellets complemented with frozen foods such as brine shrimp, tubifex worms, and bloodworms. Don't forget to occasionally treat them with blanched vegetables. Also, they might not readily eat during the day. As such, ensure that food is accessible to them during their active times.

Chapter 4: Cory Catfish

Elegant Corydoras

These corydoras exhibit a silver to gold colouration, distinguished by horizontal black dotted stripes that span from the back of the head to the tail.

Scientific Name: Corydoras elegans
Care Level: Easy
Temperament: Generally peaceful, though males may exhibit aggression towards each other
Maximum Size: 3" (7cm)
Minimum Tank Size: 40 Gallon (approx. 151 litres)
Water Conditions: 70-82° F (21-27° C), dH 2-15, pH 6.0-7.5
Diet: Omnivorous
Origin: Amazon River Basin
Aquarium Type: Community

Notes:
It's recommended to house these corydoras in groups of at least five. Compatible tank mates include characins, cyprinids, anabantids, dwarf cichlids, and other catfish species. The Elegant Corydoras is a good choice for a community aquarium due to its peaceful nature. However, avoid keeping them with larger or aggressive fish species that may see them as prey. Given their occasional male-on-male aggression, it's beneficial to create an environment with ample hiding spaces. A well-planted tank with fine substrate is ideal for their comfort and wellbeing. Their diet should primarily consist of sinking pellets and wafers. However, supplementing their meals with blanched veggies occasionally can contribute to their nutritional diversity. They will also appreciate live and frozen foods such as daphnia, brine shrimp, and bloodworms. These can be used to supplement their diet and provide variety.

Julii Corydoras

The Julii Corydoras, characterized by its mottled black dots and stripes against a silver body, is a popular addition to many home aquariums.

Scientific Name: Corydoras julii
Care Level: Easy
Temperament: Peaceful
Maximum Size: 2.5" (6cm)
Minimum Tank Size: 30 Gallons (114 litres)
Water Conditions: 68-75° F, 20-23° C, dH 2-15, pH 6.0-7.2
Diet: Omnivorous; primarily fed with high-quality sinking pellets
Origin: Amazon River Basin
Aquarium Type: Community

Notes:
Julii Corydoras are social creatures and thrive when kept in groups of five or more. They are compatible with a variety of tank mates such as characins, cyprinids, anabantids, dwarf cichlids, and other catfish species. However, avoid housing them with larger, aggressive fish that may pose a threat. These catfish favor well-planted tanks with plenty of cover and a soft, fine substrate to protect their sensitive barbels. Their primary diet should consist of high-quality sinking pellets or tablets. However, they also appreciate occasional treats of blanched vegetables and a variety of live or frozen foods. Regular dietary variation can contribute to their overall health. Ensure that the water parameters are stable and within the required range. Any sudden changes can cause stress leading to disease. They are sensitive to salt and medicines so ensure to read the instructions carefully before using them in the tank. Julii Corydoras are very social and often communicate using squeaks or chirps that can sometimes be heard by the human ear during feeding or mating.

Chapter 4: Cory Catfish

Bandit Corydoras

Also known as the Masked Cory, this species can be recognized by the distinctive black stripe across its eyes and another running along the top of its back and dorsal fin, resembling a bandit's mask.

Scientific Name: Corydoras metae
Care Level: Easy
Temperament: Peaceful
Maximum Size: 2" (5cm)
Minimum Tank Size: 20 Gallons (approximately 76 litres)
Water Conditions: 72-78° F (22-27° C), dH 2-15, pH 6.0-7.5
Diet: Omnivorous
Origin: Colombia, South America
Aquarium Type: Community

Notes:
Bandit Corydoras thrive in groups of at least 5, and can coexist harmoniously with characins, cyprinids, anabantids, dwarf cichlids, and other catfish. However, they should not be kept with large or aggressive fish. Their ideal habitat is a well-planted tank with ample cover and a fine substrate. Their diet should include good quality micro sinking pellets or flakes, supplemented with occasional blanched vegetables. They also relish treats of freeze-dried bloodworms, chopped earthworms, and brine shrimp. Bandit Corydoras are known for their active and entertaining behavior. They are often seen swimming quickly to the surface for a gulp of air, which is a normal part of their respiration. Bandit Corydoras are quite adaptable and can tolerate a variety of water parameters, although sudden changes can cause them stress. Regular water changes and good filtration will help to maintain water quality and keep these catfish healthy.

Chapter 4: Cory Catfish

Panda Corydoras

Resembling its namesake with its unique coloration, the Panda Corydoras has a black stripe across its eyes, a black dorsal fin, and a patch near its tail fin that mirror the markings of a panda.

Scientific Name: Corydoras panda
Care Level: Easy
Temperament: Peaceful bottom-dweller
Maximum Size: 2" (5cm)
Minimum Tank Size: 20 Gallons (75 litres)
Water Conditions: 70-79° F, 21-26° C, dH 2-15, pH 6.0-7.2
Diet: Omnivore
Origin: Upper Amazon River in Peru
Aquarium Type: Community

Notes:
Panda Corydoras thrive best in groups of at least 5 or more and can be housed with characins, cyprinids, anabantids, dwarf cichlids, and other catfish. Avoid keeping them with large, aggressive fish. They prefer a well-planted tank environment, with plenty of cover and fine substrate to mimic their natural habitat. Their diet should include a high-quality micro sinking pellet or flake food. This can be supplemented with blanched vegetables occasionally. They are also fond of freeze-dried bloodworms, chopped earthworms, and brine shrimp. Remember to provide a varied diet for optimum health. The Panda Corydoras is more sensitive to water conditions than other corydoras species. So, it's crucial to ensure that the water in your aquarium is clean and well-maintained. Regular water changes and proper filtration will go a long way in keeping these fish healthy. These corydoras exhibit a playful behavior, which can be quite entertaining to watch, especially when kept in groups.

Chapter 4: Cory Catfish

Peppered Corydoras

The Peppered Corydoras, also known as the mottled corydoras, is recognizable by its grey markings.

Scientific Name: Corydoras paleatus
Care Level: Easy
Temperament: Peaceful
Maximum Size: 3" (7.5cm)
Minimum Tank Size: 20 Gallons (75 liters)
Water Conditions: 72-80° F, 22-26° C, dH 2-12, pH 6.0-7.0
Diet: Omnivore
Origin: South America, specifically the Amazon region
Aquarium Type: Community

Notes:
Peppered Corydoras thrive in groups and should be kept in numbers of 5 or more. They are best suited to a well-planted aquarium that provides plenty of cover and hiding spots, along with a fine substrate to mimic their natural habitat. These fish are generally peaceful and can coexist with a variety of other non-aggressive species. For optimum health, provide them with a balanced diet that includes freeze-dried bloodworms and tubifex, sinking catfish pellets, and flake food. They also appreciate occasional treats of blanched vegetables. Regular water changes and maintaining clean conditions in the tank are essential to their well-being. Remember, like all fish, Peppered Corydoras contribute to the bioload of the tank and rely on a well-maintained filter system to remain healthy.

Chapter 4: Cory Catfish

Salt & Pepper Corydoras

The Salt & Pepper Corydoras can be recognized by its distinctive small, black, spotted markings.

Scientific Name: Corydoras habrosus
Care Level: Easy
Temperament: Peaceful
Maximum Size: 1" (2.5cm)
Minimum Tank Size: 15 Gallon (60 litre)
Water Conditions: 77-80° F, 25-26° C, dH 2-22, pH 6.0-8.0
Diet: Omnivore - A diet comprising high-quality micro pellet/flake is recommended
Origin: South America
Aquarium Type: Community

Notes:
For the Salt & Pepper Corydoras, a well-planted tank with plenty of cover and fine substrate is essential to mimic its natural habitat. These fish thrive in groups and should be kept with at least 4 other individuals. They are best housed with similar-sized, peaceful species. These fish are generally compatible with most other peaceful and bottom-dwelling species. However, due to their small size, avoid keeping them with predatory species such as the Pictus catfish or other large fish that could pose a threat. In terms of diet, these petite fish will readily accept smaller flakes and micro pellets. Ensure a varied diet for their optimal health. Like all fish, Salt & Pepper Corydoras depend on a well-maintained aquarium for their health, so regular water changes and efficient filtration are critical.

Chapter 4: Cory Catfish

Schwartz's Catfish

Schwartz's Corydoras is easily recognized by its distinctive small, horizontal black stripes set against a bright silver body.

Scientific Name: Corydoras schwartzi
Care Level: Easy
Temperament: Peaceful
Maximum Size: 2" (5cm)
Minimum Tank Size: 30 Gallons (100 litre)
Water Conditions: 72-79° F, 22-26° C, dH 2-12, pH 5.8-7.0
Diet: Omnivore
Origin: South America
Aquarium Type: Community

Notes:
Schwartz's Corydoras thrive best in groups of at least 5 or more. They are ideal for community tanks, compatible with characins, cyprinids, anabantids, dwarf cichlids, and other catfish. They prefer a well-planted aquarium environment with plenty of hiding places and fine substrate to mimic their natural habitat. A varied diet is key for their health. They should be fed small sinking pellets or wafers, supplemented with frozen foods such as brine shrimp. Additionally, occasional servings of blanched vegetables will be greatly enjoyed. Regular water changes and proper filtration are essential to maintain the clean water conditions that these fish require. Schwartz's Catfish are not only popular for their attractive appearance but also for their hardy nature and ability to help keep tanks clean by scavenging for uneaten food and algae.

Sixray Corydoras

The Sixray Corydoras, easily identifiable by its small black spots on a silver body, is indeed a small species.

Scientific Name: Corydoras leucomelas
Care Level: Easy
Temperament: Peaceful
Maximum Size: 1.5" (3.5cm)
Minimum Tank Size: 15 Gallons (60 litres)
Water Conditions: 72-78° F, 22-25° C, dH 8-12, pH 6.0-7.2
Diet: Omnivore – a balanced diet of good quality sinking small pellets or flakes is recommended
Origin: South America
Aquarium Type: Community

Notes:
The Sixray Corydoras should ideally be kept in groups of at least 5 for their social well-being, within a well-planted aquarium. The tank should have a fine substrate to prevent damage to their sensitive barbels and include plenty of hiding spots. Despite their small size, these Corydoras are compatible with most peaceful species of a similar size. Large predatory or aggressive species should be avoided, as these small fish could easily become a target. Their diet should consist of micro pellets and flakes, but can be supplemented with occasional live or frozen foods, such as daphnia, tubifex, and bloodworms. Regular feeding of vegetables such as zucchini or peas is also beneficial to their diet. These Corydoras are excellent scavengers, helping to maintain the cleanliness of the aquarium by eating leftover food. However, they should not be considered a substitute for regular maintenance and cleaning of the aquarium.

Chapter 4: Cory Catfish

Sterba's Corydoras

Sterba's Corydoras has a black body with white spots, and sometimes these spots form spotted stripes along its sides.

Scientific Name: Corydoras sterbai
Care Level: Easy
Temperament: Peaceful
Maximum Size: 3" (7cm)
Minimum Tank Size: 30 Gallons (100 liters)
Water Conditions: 70-79°F (21-26°C), dH 2-15, pH 6.0-7.8
Diet: Omnivore
Origin: Brazil, Amazon, South America
Aquarium Type: Community

Notes:
These corydoras should be kept in groups of 5 or more, as they are social creatures. They are well-suited for community tanks that include characins, cyprinids, anabantids, dwarf cichlids, and other catfish species. Provide a well-planted tank with plenty of hiding spots and fine substrate. The fine substrate helps prevent any damage to their delicate barbels. Sterba's Corydoras are omnivores and readily accept dried, flake, and frozen foods. It is essential to offer them a high-quality flake and pellet food to ensure their nutritional needs are met. Supplementing their diet with frozen brine shrimp is also beneficial. Sterba's Corydoras are known for their playful behavior and are known to be skilled jumpers, so it's essential to have a secure lid on the aquarium to prevent them from accidentally jumping out and injuring themselves.

Chapter 4: Cory Catfish

Albino Corydoras

Albino Corydoras are delightful fish, displaying a yellow to orange color with hints of red around their head.

Scientific Name: Corydoras aeneus albino
Care Level: Easy
Temperament: Peaceful
Maximum Size: 3" (7cm)
Minimum Tank Size: 25 Gallon (90 liters)
Water Conditions: 72-79°F (22-26°C), dH 2-15, pH 6.0-7.0
Diet: Omnivore – Offer a good quality sinking pellet along with frozen foods such as brine shrimp and bloodworms. They also enjoy occasional blanched vegetables.
Origin: South America
Aquarium Type: Community

Notes:
To ensure the well-being of Albino Corydoras, it's recommended to keep them in groups of about 5 or more. They are compatible with other peaceful tank mates such as tetras, barbs, livebearers, cyprinids, and dwarf cichlids, making them a great addition to a community aquarium. Provide them with a well-planted tank with plenty of hiding places and fine substrate. This setup mimics their natural environment and offers a sense of security for these social fish. Albino Corydoras are omnivores, and their primary food source should be good quality sinking pellets. To add variety and ensure their nutritional needs are met, supplement their diet with frozen foods such as brine shrimp and bloodworms. Occasional blanched vegetables can also be offered as a nutritious treat.

5 Plecos

Also known as Plecostomus, Pleco, or Plec, these fish belong to the Loricariidae family and have specially adapted mouthparts that allow them to feed on the substrate, rocks, or glass in an aquarium. They play a crucial role in algae management, as they are adept at keeping it under control.

While most Plecos are peaceful, they are predominantly bottom dwellers who prefer to rest or leisurely graze across the aquarium floor. Bear in mind that some Plecos can grow significantly large and may eventually outgrow the capacities of most home aquariums.

While they are generally peaceful, some larger species may display increased aggression with age. It is advisable to keep only one of certain species, as they can become aggressive towards each other, especially if they weren't raised together.

Additionally, be aware that some Plecos are known to damage live plants, necessitating that the plants in their tank be either artificial or of a hardy species that can withstand potential damage.

Chapter 5: Plecos

Bristlenose Pleco

The Bristlenose Pleco can be distinguished by the small bristles adorning its mouth and nose region, along with yellow or white spots speckled across a black body. There are also albino Bristlenose Plecos that are orange or yellow, as well as a few other species.

Scientific Name: Ancistrus
Care Level: Easy
Temperament: Generally Peaceful
Maximum Size: 4" - 5" (10cm - 12.5cm)
Minimum Tank Size: 30 Gallons (113 litres)
Water Conditions: 74-82° F, 23-28° C, dH 6-10, pH 6.0-7.5
Diet: Predominantly Herbivore, but can be Omnivorous
Origin: South America, Amazon Basin
Aquarium Type: Community

Notes:
The Bristlenose Pleco is a delightful addition to any aquarium, thriving in environments with abundant shelter and hiding places. A preference for planted tanks and the inclusion of bogwood or driftwood is noted, as the Pleco enjoys gnawing on these, and it aids in their digestion. The Bristlenose Pleco has a particular fondness for cucumber and algae wafers, and is proficient in cleaning the tank by feeding on algae. While the Bristlenose Pleco can typically thrive on its own, it remains compatible with most other peaceful species. It should be noted, however, that this species has been known to exhibit territorial behaviors at times.

Chapter 5: Plecos

Common Pleco

Common Plecos can typically be purchased when they are about 3 inches in size, but they can grow up to a staggering 24 inches.

Scientific Name: Hypostomus plecostomus
Care Level: Moderate
Temperament: Generally peaceful but can display signs of aggression as they mature
Maximum Size: Up to 24 inches (60cm)
Minimum Tank Size: 80-100 gallons (400 litres)
Water Conditions: 74-82°F (23-27°C), dH 6-10, pH 6.0-7.5
Diet: Primarily herbivorous, but has omnivorous tendencies
Origin: South America
Aquarium Type: Non-Community

Notes:
Common Plecos, while relatively peaceful when young, can become increasingly aggressive as they age. They are best kept as solitary individuals in large aquariums. Juveniles generally make excellent community fish, but adult Plecos should be kept in a semi-aggressive tank environment, and they should never be housed with other Common Plecos due to territorial behaviors. In addition to scavenging for algae in the tank, their diet should be supplemented with algae wafers, zucchini, cucumber, lettuce, peas, melon, and other fruits or vegetables. They may also accept shrimp pellets and flake fish food. It's crucial to provide a varied diet to ensure nutritional balance. Lastly, due to their large adult size, Common Plecos produce a substantial amount of waste. This means that excellent filtration and regular water changes are even more essential to prevent buildup of toxic waste products.

Chapter 5: Plecos

Gold Nugget Pleco

The Gold Nugget Pleco, identifiable by its striking gold/yellow stripes along the edges of its dorsal and tail fins, set against a black body, is an exquisite sight in any aquarium.

Scientific Name: Baryancistrus xanthellus (L-18)
Care Level: Moderate
Temperament: Generally peaceful, but can become territorial
Maximum Size: Up to 8" (20cm)
Minimum Tank Size: 55 Gallons (208 litres)
Water Conditions: 73-80° F (23-27° C), dH 6-10, pH 6.5-7.5
Diet: Omnivore
Origin: South America, specifically the Amazon River basin
Aquarium Type: Community

Notes:
Gold Nugget Plecos are territorial, and it's advisable to keep only one per tank as they have been known to become aggressive with each other. However, they generally coexist well with other species such as characins, cichlids, and loaches in a large community tank. These fish appreciate a well-planted tank environment with plenty of hiding spots and a substrate that's either smooth or fine-grained to mimic their natural habitat. A balanced diet for a Gold Nugget Pleco should include a high-quality sinking pellet or wafer, supplemented with frozen foods such as brine shrimp, prawns, and bloodworms. They are also known to appreciate occasional treats like cucumber. Remember to provide a varied diet for optimum health.

Chapter 5: Plecos

Leopard Sailfin Pleco

The Leopard Sailfin Pleco, aptly named for its distinctive leopard-spotted body and impressively large dorsal fin, is an impressive sight in any large aquarium.

Scientific Name: Pterygoplichthys gibbiceps
Care Level: Easy
Temperament: Generally peaceful
Maximum Size: Up to 24" (60cm)
Minimum Tank Size: 80-100 Gallons (302-378 litres)
Water Conditions: 74-80° F (23-27° C), dH 6-10, pH 6.5-7.5
Diet: Omnivore
Origin: Amazon River Basin, South America
Aquarium Type: Large-Bottom-Dweller

Notes:
The Leopard Sailfin Pleco thrives best in spacious aquariums that mimic their natural environment, with a sandy or gravel substrate, large driftwood pieces, and substantial rocks. While some plants are acceptable, it's essential to note that due to their large adult size, these fish may inadvertently uproot or damage delicate plant species. To provide them with some respite from bright aquarium lights, incorporate shaded or covered areas in the aquarium design. A balanced diet for a Leopard Sailfin Pleco should include sinking flake or pellet foods, naturally occurring algae or algae wafers, and sinking carnivore pellets. They will also consume various flake, freeze-dried, and pellet foods offered to other tank mates.

Chapter 5: Plecos

Zebra Pleco

The Zebra Pleco, characterized by its beautiful black and white striped body, doesn't grow as large as other Pleco species.

Scientific Name: Hypancistrus zebra (L-46)
Care Level: Moderate
Temperament: Peaceful and timid
Maximum Size: 3.5" (8.5cm)
Minimum Tank Size: 30 Gallons (114 liters)
Water Conditions: 79-88° F (26-31° C), dH 2-6, pH 6.0-7.5
Diet: Carnivore – high-quality sinking pellets or wafers
Origin: Brazil, Xingu River
Aquarium Type: Community

Notes:
The Zebra Pleco is a shy, nocturnal species and prefers not to be housed with other bottom-dwelling fish that would compete for food and territory. Keeping them with other fish of similar temperament is advisable. Their habitat should mimic their natural environment, favoring plenty of plant cover, driftwood, and hiding places with fine substrate. Subdued lighting helps maintain their comfort and reduce stress. While the Zebra Pleco is an omnivore, it has a preference for a meat-based diet. Feed them high-quality flake food, sinking carnivore pellets, and frozen or freeze-dried foods like bloodworms, tubifex, and brine shrimp, complemented occasionally by sinking algae wafers for nutritional variety. Zebra Plecos are relatively rare and can be quite expensive due to export restrictions from their native Brazil.

Chapter 5: Plecos

Albino Sailfin Pleco

The Albino Sailfin Pleco exhibits a distinctive orange/yellow hue. Although it can potentially grow up to 24 inches in the wild, it generally only reaches half that size in a home aquarium setting.

Scientific Name: Pterygoplichthys gibbiceps var. albino
Care Level: Easy
Temperament: Generally peaceful
Maximum Size: Typically between 7" and 12" (17cm - 30cm) in captivity
Minimum Tank Size: 75 Gallons (300 litres)
Water Conditions: 69-78° F, 20-25° C, dH 6-10, pH 6.5-7.5
Diet: Primarily herbivorous
Origin: Amazon Basin, South America
Aquarium Type: Large-Bottom-Dweller

Notes:
This pleco thrives in spacious aquariums with sandy or gravel substrates, large pieces of driftwood, rocks, and some plants. The fish appreciates shaded areas within the aquarium to avoid bright lights. Due to its potential size, it can inadvertently damage or uproot sensitive plants during its swimming and foraging activities, so a carefully planned tank layout is advisable. Although primarily herbivorous, they have a varied diet consisting of sinking pellet or flake foods, naturally occurring algae, algae wafers, vegetables, and sinking carnivore pellets. The Albino Sailfin Pleco also consumes other types of flake, freeze-dried, and pellet foods provided for tank mates.

Chapter 5: Plecos

Royal Pleco

The Royal Pleco, with its captivating palette of mossy green and striking black streaks accentuating its distinct humped body, provides a remarkable sight in any aquatic setting.

Scientific Name: Panaque nigrolineatus (L-027)
Care Level: Easy
Temperament: Peaceful
Maximum Size: 12" (30cm)
Minimum Tank Size: 55 Gallons (200 litre)
Water Conditions: 74-79° F, 23-26° C, dH 6-10, pH 6.5-7.5
Diet: Xylophagous (wood-eating), supplemented with sinking pellets and occasional fresh vegetables
Origin: South America
Aquarium Type: Large-Bottom-Dweller

Notes:
Provide them with a sandy or gravel substrate, larger pieces of driftwood, and large rocks. They also appreciate the inclusion of plants, wood, or rocks that create a covered or shaded area within the aquarium, giving them respite from bright aquarium lights when needed. Although generally peaceful, the Royal Pleco can exhibit territorial behavior, especially towards other Royal Plecos or similarly-shaped fish. Ensure ample space and hiding spots to mitigate territorial disputes. Their preferred diet includes sinking flake or pellet foods, naturally occurring algae, vegetables, and importantly, wood, as they are known for their wood-eating tendencies. They can also consume other various flake, freeze-dried and pellet foods that are fed to other tank mates.

Chapter 5: Plecos

Blue Phantom Pleco

The Blue Phantom Pleco, boasting blue and white spots on its dark grey body, hails from the Orinoco River Basin in Venezuela.

Scientific Name: Hemiancistrus sp. (L-128)
Care Level: Moderate
Temperament: Peaceful
Maximum Size: 7" (17cm)
Minimum Tank Size: 30 Gallons (115 litres)
Water Conditions: 72-77° F, 22-25° C, dH 6-16, pH 6.0-7.5
Diet: Omnivore
Origin: South America
Aquarium Type: Community

Notes:
The Blue Phantom Pleco thrives in an environment with sandy or gravel substrate and appreciates the presence of large pieces of driftwood and rocks. Incorporating plants into the tank setup helps create shaded areas for this species to retreat from bright aquarium lights when necessary. They generally exhibit compatibility with most other peaceful species, making them suitable for a community tank setup. Their diet should consist of a variety of foods, including sinking flake or pellet foods, naturally occurring algae or algae wafers, vegetables, sinking carnivore pellets, as well as other types of flake, freeze-dried, and pellet foods shared with tank mates. he Blue Phantom Pleco is a moderately challenging species to keep due to its preference for high-quality water conditions. Regular water changes, sufficient filtration, and the maintenance of proper water parameters are crucial for this species.

Chapter 5: Plecos

Clown Pleco

The Clown Pleco, characterized by its distinct yellow stripes on a black-brown body, is a native of South America.

Scientific Name: Panaque maccus (L-162)
Care Level: Easy
Temperament: Peaceful
Maximum Size: 4" (10cm)
Minimum Tank Size: 30 Gallons (113 litres)
Water Conditions: 75-82° F (24-28°C), dH 6-10, pH 6.5-7.5
Diet: Primarily herbivore, but will eat some protein-based foods
Origin: South America
Aquarium Type: Community

Notes:
These plecos prefer a habitat that includes a sandy or gravel substrate. They appreciate areas in the aquarium that are shaded by plants, driftwood, or rocks, which provide cover from bright lights. They tend to be compatible with most other peaceful species, making them a good choice for a community aquarium. Their diet primarily consists of wood, so driftwood should be included in the tank for them to gnaw on. While they also appreciate vegetables and high-quality plant-based sinking pellets or wafers, they will eat some protein-based foods, such as sinking carnivore pellets and occasional offerings of freeze-dried or live foods like bloodworms or brine shrimp. However, wood should form the staple of their diet as they cannot digest other foods as efficiently.

6

Other Catfish

Characterized by their distinctive barbels, which strikingly echo a cat's whiskers, catfish are primarily bottom dwellers. These social creatures typically thrive in groups, relishing environments rich with fine gravel and an abundance of hideaways.

Many species of catfish are nocturnal, meaning they're most active during the night. Therefore, having a dimly lit or shaded area in the aquarium can mimic their natural habitat and keep them comfortable.

These fish tend to have a broad diet, consuming everything from algae and plants to insects and other small aquatic animals, depending on the species. In captivity, their diet should be tailored to their specific needs to ensure optimal health and longevity.

Lastly, while many catfish are peaceful, some species can be territorial or aggressive. Therefore, it's crucial to research and understand the particular behavioral traits of the species you are considering before introducing them to a community tank.

With their unique appearances and behaviors, catfish can add an interesting dynamic to your tank if their specific needs are met.

Chapter 6: Other Catfish

Otocinclus Catfish

The Otocinclus Catfish, also known as the "Oto," is a small, industrious fish known for its exceptional algae-eating abilities. With a black stripe running lengthwise across its silver-gray body and a small sucker-like mouth, this fish is easily distinguishable.

Scientific Name: Otocinclus affinis
Care Level: Easy
Temperament: Peaceful
Maximum Size: 2" (5cm)
Minimum Tank Size: 20 Gallons (80 litres)
Water Conditions: 70-79° F (21-26° C), dH 6-10, pH 6.0-7.2
Diet: Primarily Herbivore - supplement diet with high-quality algae wafers
Origin: South America
Aquarium Type: Community

Notes:
The Otocinclus is a charming and practical addition to any freshwater aquarium, renowned for its ceaseless grazing on algae. This species thrives in a well-planted aquarium furnished with hiding spots, such as rocks and driftwood. For their wellbeing, it's advisable to keep them in groups of 3 or more as they are schooling fish. While the Otocinclus Catfish will graze on algae, it's crucial to supplement their diet with high-quality algae wafers, vegetable-based flakes, or pellet food to ensure optimal health. Due to their small size and peaceful nature, they can sometimes be bullied or outmatched for food by larger or more aggressive fish. Therefore, it's best to keep them with other peaceful, community-oriented species.

Chapter 6: Other Catfish

Panda Garra

The Panda Garra, recognized for its distinctive banding of dark brown and yellow, adds vibrant flair to any community aquarium.

Scientific Name: Garra flavatra
Care Level: Moderate
Temperament: Peaceful
Maximum Size: 3" (7.6cm)
Minimum Tank Size: 30 Gallons (114 liters)
Water Conditions: 72-77° F (22-25° C), dH 6-10, pH 6.5-7.5
Diet: Omnivorous
Origin: Indonesia
Aquarium Type: Community

Notes:
The Panda Garra is an ideal addition to any peaceful community aquarium. It is best kept in groups of three or more to promote social interaction and natural behavior. These fish thrive in well-planted aquariums with ample hiding spaces, a fine substrate, and moderate lighting. They enjoy a strong current, so equipping your filter with a power head is recommended to mimic their natural habitat. As omnivores, Panda Garras enjoy a varied diet. Prepared algae flakes or wafers should form the base of their diet, supplemented by frozen or freeze-dried foods. Occasional treats of bloodworms or tubifex worms are also recommended, as well as blanched veggies for additional nutritional diversity. A slice of cucumber now and then can serve as a much-enjoyed treat.

Chapter 6: Other Catfish

Pictus Catfish

The Pictus Catfish is easily recognizable by its dark black spots on a white or grey body and strikingly long barbels, akin to whiskers.

Scientific Name: Pimelodus pictus
Care Level: Moderate
Temperament: Generally Peaceful; may prey on smaller fish
Maximum Size: 6" (15cm)
Minimum Tank Size: 55 Gallons (208 liters)
Water Conditions: 71-81° F (22-27° C), dH 6-10, pH 6.0-7.5
Diet: Omnivorous; prefers sinking pellets
Origin: Amazon River Basin
Aquarium Type: Community

Notes:
While Pictus Catfish are captivating when small, they can grow considerably larger. Their mouth size is deceptive; they can open wide enough to consume smaller fish such as neon tetras or guppies. Compatible tankmates include rainbowfish, medium to large-sized characins, cyprinids, and robust catfish like Loricariids or Doradids. Pictus Catfish appreciate a dimly lit, heavily planted tank equipped with an abundance of rocks, caves, and driftwood. Hardy plant varieties are recommended due to the catfish's active nature. These fish are primarily nocturnal and may exhibit predatory behavior, but they generally coexist well with similarly sized species. Diet should include sinking pellets or wafers, supplemented with treats like frozen bloodworms. When handling Pictus Catfish, extreme care should be taken as they have sharp pectoral and dorsal spines which can cause injury.

Chapter 6: Other Catfish

Whiptail Catfish

Depending on the exact species the Whiptail Catfish are typically a dark brown or greenish color, with patterns that can include spots, bands, or stripes depending on the specific species. Their bodies are covered with bony plates for protection, which gives them a slightly armored appearance. As their common name suggests, they have a lengthy, whip-like tail.

Scientific Name: Rineloricaria sp.
Care Level: Easy
Temperament: Peaceful
Maximum Size: 5" (12cm)
Minimum Tank Size: 55 Gallon (200 litres)
Water Conditions: 68-77° F, 20-25° C, dH 4-10, pH 6.5-7.0
Diet: Omnivore
Origin: Brazil
Aquarium Type: Community

Notes:
Known for their peaceable nature and intriguing appearance, Whiptail Catfish remain relatively small and robust, making them an excellent choice for community aquariums inhabited by other non-aggressive species. They thrive in well-planted aquariums that offer abundant cover and a fine substrate, paired with diffused lighting. These catfish have a fondness for algae and bogwood. Their diet should consist of a variety of vegetable-based foods such as lettuce, peas, courgette/zucchini, and blanched spinach, in addition to a high-quality sinking pellet food. They also readily graze on algae present in the tank.

Chapter 6: Other Catfish

Featherfin Catfish

Also known as the Featherfin Squeaker or Lace Catfish, this species typically showcases a light brown body adorned with dark spots, as well as a set of long barbels reminiscent of whiskers.

Scientific Name: Synodontis eupterus
Care Level: Easy
Temperament: Peaceful
Maximum Size: 6" (15cm)
Minimum Tank Size: 55 Gallon (200 litre)
Water Conditions: 68-77° F, 20-25° C, dH 8-10, pH 6.5-7.0
Diet: Omnivore
Origin: Africa
Aquarium Type: Community

Notes:
Though generally peaceful, the Featherfin Catfish tends to exhibit a somewhat boisterous behavior and, therefore, best thrives when housed with medium to large-sized fish or others of its size. This species greatly appreciates an abundance of dark hiding places to retreat to. When selecting a substrate, ensure it is fine and devoid of any sharp bits, as these could potentially injure the catfish's sensitive barbels. Well-suited to life in a home aquarium, the Featherfin Catfish is a creature full of character. The diet should include sinking pellets as well as live or frozen foods. They are strong swimmers and will often be seen darting across the tank, especially when young. As they age, they tend to be a bit more sedentary but still require plenty of space. It's important to note that the Featherfin Catfish is known to be a bit of a jumper, so a well-fitted tank lid is recommended to prevent any unexpected escapes.

Chapter 6: Other Catfish

Striped Raphael

The Striped Raphael, also known as the Thorny or Talking Catfish, is renowned for producing distinctive clicking and squeaking sounds.

Scientific Name: Platydoras armatulus
Care Level: Easy (spiky fins require careful handling)
Temperament: Peaceful
Maximum Size: 7" (18cm)
Minimum Tank Size: 40 Gallons (150 litres)
Water Conditions: 75-80°F, 23-26°C, dH 4-10, pH 6.5-7.0
Diet: Omnivore
Origin: Colombia
Aquarium Type: Community

Notes:
The Striped Raphael is generally compatible with a broad range of species, but any fish small enough to fit in its mouth should be avoided as tank mates. This species is fond of burrowing, so it is best to provide a fine sand substrate and an abundance of hiding spots within the tank. The Striped Raphael catfish is quite fond of sinking catfish pellets but should also be provided with a varied diet to ensure optimal health. Live or frozen foods can be a great supplement to their diet. These fish are nocturnal and can be quite active during the night. Therefore, it's important to ensure their habitat has sufficient cover for them to hide during the day. Take care when netting these fish or performing maintenance in your tank, as their spines can get entangled in net material and their fins can cause slight injury if not handled properly

Chapter 6: Other Catfish

Banjo Catfish

The Banjo Catfish, aptly named for its unique banjo-like shape, boasts a predominantly brown coloration and a distinctly elongated tail.

Scientific Name: Bunocephalus coracoideus
Care Level: Moderate
Temperament: Peaceful
Maximum Size: 6" (15cm)
Minimum Tank Size: 55 Gallons (200 liters)
Water Conditions: 68-77° F, 20-25° C, dH 8-19, pH 6.5-8.0
Diet: Omnivore
Origin: Brazil
Aquarium Type: Community

Notes:
The Banjo Catfish appreciates a soft sandy substrate which allows it to exhibit its natural burrowing behavior. Offering a setting with subdued lighting and an abundance of hiding places, including pieces of bogwood and cavernous structures, will provide an ideal environment for this fish. When considering cohabitation, the Banjo Catfish is generally compatible with a variety of peaceful species, including Tetras, Cichlids, Corydoras, and Loaches. Also, while the Banjo Catfish is known to be a peaceful species, it is important to be aware that small fish could be eaten if they fit into the Banjo Catfish's mouth, so tank mates should be chosen wisely. It can thrive either as a solitary specimen or in a group, making it a versatile addition to a community aquarium.

7 Characins

Belonging to the Characidae family, Characins are vibrant and energetic schooling fish that seamlessly integrate into peaceful community aquariums. These fish thrive when in groups, ideally consisting of six or more of the same species, resulting in impressive and dynamic visual displays within the aquarium.

The ideal habitat for Characins is a meticulously planted aquarium under moderate lighting, which not only mimics their natural habitat, but also provides them with sufficient hiding spots and room to explore. This combination allows them to exhibit their best colours and behaviours.

These fish prefer soft, slightly acidic water, which can be achieved by the addition of peat to the filter or use of blackwater extracts.

It's important to remember, too, that although Characins are generally peaceful, they can sometimes nip at the fins of slow-moving or long-finned tankmates, especially when kept in too-small groups or if they're not provided with sufficient space. As such, careful selection of tankmates and appropriate stocking levels are critical.

Chapter 7: Characins

Black Phantom Tetra

The Black Phantom Tetra boasts a light grey body accentuated by an eye-catching black patch, encased by a ring of shimmering silver.

Scientific Name: Hyphessobrycon megalopterus
Care Level: Easy
Temperament: Peaceful
Maximum Size: 1.5" (4cm)
Minimum Tank Size: 15 Gallons (60 litre)
Water Conditions: 72-82° F, 22-28° C, dH 4-8, pH 6.0-7.5
Diet: Omnivore – a high-quality flake food is recommended
Origin: Brazil
Aquarium Type: Community

Notes:
Black Phantom Tetras thrive best when housed in schools of six or more, as this mirrors their natural social structures and helps reduce stress. They have a preference for aquariums with abundant vegetation and ample hiding spaces. These tetras get along well with other docile tropical species of similar size and temperament. When cohabitating with barb species like tiger barbs, it's critical to keep them in groups, as barbs have a tendency to nip at each other in a display of natural behavior. Their dietary regimen should include high-quality flake food, supplemented with brine shrimp, daphnia, freeze-dried tubifex or blood worms, and micro pellets to ensure balanced nutrition. Although Black Phantom Tetras are peaceful by nature, they can display territorial behaviors, especially the males towards each other. This is especially true when they are kept in smaller groups or pairs. Therefore, maintaining them in larger groups can help dilute any aggression and create a more harmonious tank environment.

Chapter 7: Charancins

Black Neon Tetra

Adorned with parallel, horizontal stripes of shimmering white and black, punctuated by subtle hints of red and yellow, the Black Neon Tetra brings a captivating charm to any aquarium.

Scientific Name: Hyphessobrycon herbertaxelrodi
Care Level: Easy
Temperament: Peaceful
Maximum Size: 1.5" (4cm)
Minimum Tank Size: 12 Gallons (50 litres)
Water Conditions: 72-79° F, 22-26° C, dH 4-8, pH 5.5-7.0
Diet: Omnivorous
Origin: Brazilian Amazon
Aquarium Type: Community

Notes:
The Black Neon Tetra thrives in schools, and it's recommended to maintain at least a quintet for their wellbeing. Suitable tank companions include other tetra species, hatchet fish, cory cats, rasbora, gourami, peaceful barb species, and smaller cichlids such as rams cichlids. Despite their serene demeanor, these tetras may struggle to hold their own against boisterous species like barbs and danios when it comes to securing food and territory. Moreover, their diminutive adult size makes them an ill-suited choice for cohabitation with larger aquarium inhabitants such as angelfish, shark, or bigger catfish species, which could perceive the tetras as nocturnal snacks. In terms of habitat, they will appreciate a well-planted tank with ample hiding spots. They have a diverse palate and will gladly accept an array of flake, crisp, freeze-dried, and frozen foods.

Chapter 7: Characins

Bleeding Heart Tetra

Identifiable by its signature red patch near the pectoral fins and a contrasting black and white patch on the dorsal fin, the Bleeding Heart Tetra is a unique and fascinating addition to any aquarium.

Scientific Name: Hyphessobrycon erythrostigma
Care Level: Easy
Temperament: Peaceful
Maximum Size: 2" (5cm)
Minimum Tank Size: 20 Gallons (80 litres)
Water Conditions: 73-81° F, 22-27° C, dH 4-10, pH 5.5-7.0
Diet: Omnivorous
Origin: Amazon Basin (Brazil, Peru, Colombia)
Aquarium Type: Community

Notes:
Bleeding Heart Tetras thrive best in larger schools of five or more. A well-planted tank with abundant cover enhances their habitat, mimicking their natural environment. Their cohabitants should be similarly peaceful tropical community species, including tranquil bottom dwellers and non-aggressive dwarf cichlid species. Although they are generally peaceful, they may nip at the fins of slow moving fish or fish with long, flowing fins. So, it's better to avoid keeping them with such species. A balanced diet for these fish includes a variety of flake, crisp, freeze-dried, and frozen foods. As with many tetra species, the Bleeding Heart Tetra appreciates a tank with soft, slightly acidic water. They are a great candidate for a blackwater aquarium, which imitates their natural Amazonian habitat.

Chapter 7: Characins

Blood-fin Tetra

Recognizable by its distinct red fins contrasting with a silver body, the Blood-fin Tetra is a striking species.

Scientific Name: Aphyocharax anisitsi
Care Level: Easy
Temperament: Generally peaceful, but may be fin nippers
Maximum Size: 2" (5cm)
Minimum Tank Size: 20 Gallons (80 liters)
Water Conditions: 64-82° F (18-28° C), dH 2-30, pH 6.0-8.0
Diet: Omnivore
Origin: South America, primarily in Argentina, Brazil, and Paraguay
Aquarium Type: Community

Notes:
The Blood-fin Tetra thrives in schools of at least 6 individuals, contributing to a visually stunning display in the aquarium. They appreciate a well-planted tank with plenty of hiding spots, mimicking their natural habitat. Suitable tank mates should be similarly sized, peaceful species. These tetras are generally peaceful but can sometimes nip at the fins of long-finned or slower fish. Therefore, caution should be exercised when selecting tank mates. As omnivores, Blood-fin Tetras appreciate a diverse diet. Feed them a mix of high-quality flake food, freeze-dried, and frozen foods. Periodic inclusion of live foods can also contribute to their overall health and color vibrancy. It's also worth noting that Blood-fin Tetras, like other tetras, prefer soft, slightly acidic water which resembles their natural habitat. Also, they are mid-dwelling fish, so they will usually spend most of their time in the middle layer of the water column

Chapter 7: Characins

Buenos Aires Tetra

Recognized by its silver body, red-tipped fins, and a black marking on the tail fin, this tetra is a distinctive presence in an aquarium.

Scientific Name: Hyphessobrycon anisitsi
Care Level: Easy
Temperament: Generally peaceful but can display minor aggression
Maximum Size: 3" (7.5cm)
Minimum Tank Size: 30 Gallons (113 litres)
Water Conditions: 64-82° F, 18-28° C, dH 12-35, pH 7.0-8.5
Diet: Omnivore
Origin: South America
Aquarium Type: Community

Notes:
Buenos Aires Tetras exhibit slightly more aggression compared to smaller tetra species, but usually remain peaceful towards fish of a similar size. They have a tendency to nibble on certain types of aquatic plants, so while they may not cause significant harm to a thriving, well-established planted aquarium, this aspect should be considered when planning the tank environment. Keeping them in a group of at least 5 will promote their social behavior and reduce any potential aggressiveness. They thrive in a well-planted tank with ample cover. Their diet can be diversified with a variety of flake, crisp, freeze-dried, and frozen foods, which they will readily accept. These fish are hearty eaters but overfeeding can pollute the water and cause health issues. Feed them small amounts 1-2 times a day, and only give as much as they can eat within a few minutes.

Chapter 7: Charcins

Congo Tetra

The Congo Tetra is known for its vibrant blue, red, and yellow-gold coloring. This tetra transitions from blue on its upper part to red in the middle, then to yellow-gold, and back to red just above the belly.

Scientific Name: Phenacogrammus interruptus
Care Level: Moderate
Temperament: Peaceful
Maximum Size: 3" (7cm)
Minimum Tank Size: 30 Gallons (100 litre)
Water Conditions: 74-84° F (23-28° C), dH 4-10, pH 6.0-7.5
Diet: Omnivore
Origin: Congo River Basin, Africa
Family: Alestidae
Aquarium Type: Community

Notes:
Congo Tetras should ideally be kept in groups of at least six, as they are schooling fish. They are best viewed in a well-lit tank that allows their colors to shine. For a healthy gender balance, it is recommended to keep two or three females for every male. Alternatively, an all-male group can be maintained. Provide these fish with a well-planted tank that offers plenty of cover. Congo Tetras enjoy a varied diet and will readily accept a mix of flake, crisp, freeze-dried, and frozen foods. Also, keep in mind that due to their larger size compared to other tetra species, they require a bit more space to swim comfortably. It is worth noting that Congo Tetras are not as robust as some other Tetra species and can be more sensitive to water quality.

Chapter 7: Characins

Emperor Tetra

The Emperor Tetra is characterized by its three-pronged tail and a prominent black stripe running along the length of its body.

Scientific Name: Nematobrycon palmeri
Care Level: Easy
Temperament: Peaceful
Maximum Size: 2" (5cm)
Minimum Tank Size: 30 Gallons (100 liters)
Water Conditions: 74-82° F (23-27° C), dH 4-10, pH 5.5-7.0
Diet: Omnivore
Origin: Rio San Juan, Rio Atrato, Colombia
Aquarium Type: Community

Notes:
Despite their size, Emperor Tetras are peaceful and can comfortably coexist with angelfish, gouramis, smaller catfish, and certain shark species. Their non-aggressive nature also makes them suitable tank mates for smaller or more delicate fish. It's advisable to keep Emperor Tetras in groups of at least five. They appreciate a well-planted aquarium that offers plenty of hiding spots. Emperor Tetras have diverse dietary preferences, readily accepting a variety of foods, including flake, crisp, freeze-dried, and frozen options. Ensuring a balanced and varied diet will contribute to their overall health and vibrancy. The Emperor Tetra can exhibit brighter colors and more active behaviors if the aquarium has a darker substrate and background. This can be a wonderful visual effect and can also help the fish feel more secure.

Chapter 7: Charcins

Glowlight Tetra

The Glowlight Tetra, characterized by its silver color and distinctive bright, iridescent orange to red stripe running across its body, is an attractive addition to any freshwater aquarium.

Scientific Name: Hemigrammus erythrozonus
Care Level: Easy
Temperament: Peaceful
Maximum Size: 2" (5cm)
Minimum Tank Size: 10 Gallons (40 liters)
Water Conditions: 72-78° F (22-25° C), dH 4-8, pH 5.5-7.0
Diet: Omnivore
Origin: South America
Aquarium Type: Community

Notes:
Glowlight Tetras thrive in community aquariums with other small to medium-sized peaceful species. As schooling fish, it's best to keep them in groups of at least 5, which will also enhance their vibrant coloring and natural behavior. Their bright orange-red stripe will become more vibrant, especially against a dark substrate or background. These fish appreciate a well-planted tank with plenty of cover, imitating their natural habitat and providing spaces to hide. For their diet, Glowlight Tetras will readily accept a balanced variety of flake, crisp, freeze-dried, and frozen foods, ensuring they receive all the nutrients they need. Avoid pairing Glowlight Tetras with large or aggressive fish species, as they can become targets due to their small size and vibrant colors.

Chapter 7: Charancins

Golden Pristella Tetra

Golden Pristella Tetra, also known as the X-ray fish, boasts a semi-translucent body adorned with black and yellow markings on its dorsal fin.

Scientific Name: Pristella maxillaris
Care Level: Easy
Temperament: Peaceful
Maximum Size: 2" (5cm)
Minimum Tank Size: 10 Gallons (40 liters)
Water Conditions: 72-79°F (22-26°C), dH 4-8, pH 5.5-7.0
Diet: Omnivore
Origin: Brazilian Amazon
Aquarium Type: Community

Notes:
Golden Pristella Tetras are ideal for tranquil community aquariums. They are not suited for cohabitation with semi-aggressive species such as angelfish, catfish, and barbs, or any fish large enough to pose a predation threat. These fish are most striking when maintained in sizable schools of at least six individuals. To replicate their natural habitat, provide them with a well-planted tank that affords ample hiding spots. Golden Pristella Tetras exhibit an omnivorous diet. A variety of flake, crisp, freeze-dried, and frozen foods will ensure their nutritional needs are adequately met. It is also important to note that Golden Pristella Tetras thrive in a slightly acidic to neutral pH environment, and in softer water, reflecting the conditions of their native habitat in the Amazon. These tetras are known for their resilience, making them a good choice for beginner aquarists.

Chapter 7: Characins

Lemon Tetra

The Lemon Tetra, distinguished by its translucent yellow body and black and yellow-marked fins, adds a vibrant touch to any aquarium.

Scientific Name: Hyphessobrycon pulchripinnis
Care Level: Easy
Temperament: Peaceful
Maximum Size: 2" (5cm)
Minimum Tank Size: 20 Gallons (75 litre)
Water Conditions: 72-79° F (22-26° C), dH 4-8, pH 5.5-7.0
Diet: Omnivore
Origin: Brazilian Amazon
Aquarium Type: Community

Notes:
Lemon Tetras are suitable for peaceful community aquariums that do not house semi-aggressive species such as angelfish, catfish, or barbs, nor larger fish that could potentially eat them. These fish are social and display their best behaviors and colors when kept in schools of at least six. Their vibrant hues can make for a spectacular display, especially in a well-planted tank with plenty of hiding spots. Ensure a secure tank cover, as these fish have been known to jump when startled or during feeding times. Lemon Tetras readily accept a varied diet, including flake food, crisps, freeze-dried, and frozen foods. Offering a diverse diet will ensure they receive the necessary nutrients for their health and coloration. Be mindful of their light requirements. They prefer subdued lighting or a naturally lit room without direct sunlight. Too much light can stress them out and cause health problems.

Chapter 7: Characins

Neon Tetra

This tetra is identified by its light-blue back over a silver-white abdomen and a distinctive blue and red stripe along its side.

Scientific Name: Paracheirodon innesi
Care Level: Easy
Temperament: Peaceful
Maximum Size: 1.5" (4cm)
Minimum Tank Size: 10 Gallons (40 litres)
Water Conditions: 72-79° F (22-26° C), dH 4-8, pH 5.5-7.0
Diet: Omnivore
Origin: Amazon Basin, Brazil
Aquarium Type: Community

Notes:
Neon Tetras are suitable only for very peaceful community aquariums, avoiding semi-aggressive species like angelfish, certain catfish, and barbs or larger fish that could potentially eat the Neons. These fish form a spectacular display when kept in large groups, with a minimum of 5 recommended. For an exceptionally colourful display, consider housing 20 or more in a larger tank. A well-planted tank with plenty of cover will make an ideal home for these small, active fish. They readily accept a variety of foods, including flakes, crisps, freeze-dried, and frozen foods. Variety in their diet will contribute to their overall health and vibrant colouration. Although Neon Tetras are generally hardy, they can be sensitive to sudden changes in water parameters. Therefore, gradual acclimatization is essential when first introducing them to a new aquarium.

Chapter 7: Characins

Penguin Tetra

The Penguin Tetras, characterized by their pale gold hue, and a black stripe across their bodies that extends into the lower half of the tail fin.

Scientific Name: Thayeria boehlkei
Care Level: Easy
Temperament: Mostly Peaceful, but can exhibit occasional aggression and fin-nipping
Maximum Size: 3" (7cm)
Minimum Tank Size: 20 Gallons (80 liters)
Water Conditions: 64-82° F (16-27° C), dH 4-8, pH 5.8-8.5
Diet: Omnivore
Origin: South America, Amazon Basin
Aquarium Type: Community

Notes:
Penguin Tetras should be maintained in groups of at least 5 to thrive and are active swimmers, so it's essential to provide enough swimming space in the aquarium. A well-planted tank with ample cover is recommended to mimic their natural habitat and provide them with comfort. They appreciate a dimly lit environment with soft, slightly acidic water. Avoid pairing them with large-finned fish such as Bettas and Guppies, as Penguin Tetras might not resist the temptation to nip at their tail fins. Their diet can include a variety of flake, crisp, freeze-dried, and frozen foods, which they will readily accept. Regular water changes and maintenance are crucial to ensure their well-being, as they can be sensitive to poor water conditions.

Chapter 7: Charancins

Red-eye Tetra

The Red-eye Tetra is characterized by its bright silver body, complemented by a black basal half of the tail bordered by white, and a distinctive thin red circle around its eye.

Scientific Name: Moenkhausia sanctaefilomenae
Care Level: Easy
Temperament: Peaceful
Maximum Size: 3" (7.5 cm)
Minimum Tank Size: 20 Gallons (75 liters)
Water Conditions: 72-80° F (22-26° C), dH 4-8, pH 6.0-8.0
Diet: Omnivore
Origin: Brazil, Paraguay, and Argentina
Aquarium Type: Community

Notes:
The Red-eye Tetra thrives when kept in a group of at least 5, as they are schooling fish. They appreciate a well-planted tank with plenty of hiding spots and swimming spaces. Typically, this fish will peacefully coexist with most other community fish species. They have a broad diet and will readily accept a variety of flake, crisp, freeze-dried, and frozen foods. Ensure regular water changes to maintain optimum water quality. While they are peaceful, they can be somewhat boisterous, especially when in large groups. This can sometimes stress more timid or slow-moving fish, so keep this in mind when selecting tank mates. Despite their hardiness, the Red-eye Tetra prefers soft, slightly acidic water that mimics their natural Amazon river habitat.

Chapter 7: Charactins

Red Phantom Tetra

The Red Phantom Tetra, known for its round black spot behind the gill plate and a black band on the dorsal fin bordered by creamy-white, is a peaceful fish that can add great beauty to any community aquarium.

Scientific Name: Hyphessobrycon sweglesi
Care Level: Easy
Temperament: Peaceful
Maximum Size: 2" (5cm)
Minimum Tank Size: 20 Gallons (80 litres)
Water Conditions: 72-82° F (22-27° C), dH 4-8, pH 6.0-7.5
Diet: Omnivore – they appreciate a well-balanced diet including high-quality flake food, brine shrimp, daphnia, freeze-dried tubifex, blood worms and micro pellets.
Origin: Brazil
Aquarium Type: Community

Notes:
Red Phantom Tetras should be kept in schools of at least 6, which helps them feel secure and encourages their natural behavior. They thrive in a well-planted tank with ample hiding spaces. They make ideal tankmates for other peaceful tropical species of similar size and temperament. While they can be kept with fin-nipping species like tiger barbs, it's important to ensure the barbs are also kept in a sizable group to keep them occupied with each other rather than harassing the tetras. These fish appreciate a well-balanced diet. They will readily accept high-quality flake food and enjoy the occasional treat of live or freeze-dried foods such as brine shrimp, daphnia, tubifex worms, or blood worms. Offering a varied diet will help keep these fish healthy and vibrant.

Chapter 7: Charancins

Rummy Nose Tetra

The Rummy Nose Tetra is a unique torpedo-shaped fish, recognizable by its black and white tail markings and distinctive bright red coloration around its mouth and eyes.

Scientific Name: Hemigrammus rhodostomus
Care Level: Easy
Temperament: Peaceful
Maximum Size: 2" (5cm)
Minimum Tank Size: 20 Gallons (80 litres)
Water Conditions: 72-77° F (22-25° C), dH 2-6, pH 5.5-7.0
Diet: Omnivore
Origin: South America
Aquarium Type: Community

Notes:
Rummy Nose Tetras thrive in an environment that replicates their natural habitat. This includes an aquarium with ample vegetation, as well as roots and other forms of driftwood for them to explore. Although attractive individually, Rummy Nose Tetras truly shine when kept in good-sized groups of 8 or more. Their synchronized swimming behavior in large groups can create a stunning display. They're peaceful by nature, making them compatible with most community fish species. As always, be sure to select tankmates of similar size and temperament to avoid potential conflicts. These omnivorous fish will readily accept a diverse diet. Offer a variety of flake, crisp, freeze-dried, and frozen foods to ensure they receive all necessary nutrients. The occasional inclusion of live food can also be beneficial for their health and coloration.

Chapter 7: Charcins

Serpae Tetra

The Serpae Tetra, also known as the Long Fin Red Minor Tetra, Long Fin Serpae Tetra, and Long Fin Blood Tetra, is a vividly colored species that stands out for its rich red body and distinctive black spot near its eye.

Scientific Name: Hyphessobrycon serpae
Care Level: Easy
Temperament: Generally peaceful, but can be fin nippers
Maximum Size: 2" (5cm)
Minimum Tank Size: 20 Gallons (80 litres)
Water Conditions: 72-82° F (22-27° C), dH 4-8, pH 6.0-7.5
Diet: Omnivore
Origin: South America
Aquarium Type: Community

Notes
Serpae Tetras thrive when kept in groups of at least 5, as this allows them to display their natural schooling behaviour. A well-planted tank with plenty of cover is recommended, which can mimic their natural Amazonian habitat and provide them with a sense of security. While generally peaceful, Serpae Tetras have been known to nip at the fins of certain species, such as guppies and betta fish. Ensure you choose tank mates that can coexist peacefully, preferably avoiding species with long or flowing fins. These fish are omnivorous and not particularly fussy eaters. They will readily accept a wide variety of foods, including flake, crisp, freeze-dried, and frozen options. To maintain optimal health and coloration, provide them with a balanced diet that includes a mix of these foods.

Chapter 7: Characins

Silver Dollar

The Silver Dollar is a unique and visually appealing species, notable for its bright silver color, broad flat body, and pale fins.

Scientific Name: Metynnis argenteus
Temperament: Generally peaceful, may exhibit aggression during feeding
Maximum Size: 6" (15cm)
Minimum Tank Size: 55 Gallons (200 litres)
Water Conditions: 72-77° F (22-25° C), dH 4-8, pH 5.0-7.0
Diet: Primarily herbivorous
Origin: South America
Aquarium Type: Community

Notes:
Silver Dollars are lively and prefer to be in schools; it is recommended to keep them in groups of five or more. This allows them to express their natural social behaviors. They thrive in tanks that replicate their natural habitat. Providing plenty of rocks, plants, and driftwood can provide them with a sense of security and opportunities for exploration. Be sure to incorporate hiding places into the setup where they can retreat if needed. While Silver Dollars are generally peaceful, they might attempt to eat smaller fish that can fit in their mouths. Select tank mates that are of similar size or larger. Despite being primarily herbivorous, they will readily accept a variety of food types. Providing a balanced diet that includes flake, crisp, freeze-dried, and frozen foods, in addition to plant-based foods, will help to keep them healthy and vibrant.

8 Labyrinth Fish

Labyrinth fish, or anabantoids, are surface air breathers belonging to the Osphronemidae family. They are named after their labyrinth organ, are a unique family of fish that have the ability to breathe air. This organ, which is highly vascularized, is an extension of their gills and allows these fish to survive in low-oxygen environments that might be inhospitable to other fish.

Labyrinth fish, are especially popular in the aquarium hobby due to their interesting behaviors and striking appearances. Gouramis, a common type of labyrinth fish, can make excellent additions to a community aquarium thanks to their vibrant colours and diverse patterns.

However, while many labyrinth fish are peaceful and can coexist with other peaceful species, some larger species are semi-aggressive. These larger labyrinth fish often have unique colorations and are graceful swimmers. They can bring a dynamic element to a community aquarium but need to be kept with other species that can tolerate their more assertive behavior.

Chapter 8: Labyrinth Fish

Chocolate Gourami

The Chocolate Gourami, characterised by its dark brown body adorned with golden bands running down its sides, is a visually appealing addition to aquariums.

Scientific Name: Sphaerichthys osphromenoides
Care Level: Advanced, due to susceptibility to disease and delicate nature
Temperament: Peaceful
Maximum Size: 3" (7cm)
Minimum Tank Size: 30 Gallons (100 litre)
Water Conditions: 75-86° F, 24-30° C, dH 1-5, pH 4.0-6.5
Diet: Omnivore
Origin: South-East Asia
Aquarium Type: Community

Notes:
The Chocolate Gourami is particularly delicate, with a high susceptibility to bacterial infections and skin parasites, underscoring the need for impeccable water quality. These fish flourish in a well-established, densely vegetated tank with a dark substrate, and they require regular water changes. Best kept in pairs, they cohabit peacefully with other non-aggressive species. In terms of diet, provide them with algae-based flake food supplemented with freeze-dried bloodworms, tubifex worms, and brine shrimp. To keep them in peak health, include a variety of high-quality fresh or frozen foods in their diet. Feed them an algae-based flake food, along with freeze-dried bloodworms, tubifex, and brine shrimp.

Chapter 8: Labyrinth Fish

Dwarf Gourami

The Dwarf Gourami is notable for its striking vertical stripes of alternating blue and red colours, while the females exhibit a more subtle silvery hue.

Scientific Name: Trichogaster lalius
Care Level: Easy
Temperament: Peaceful
Maximum Size: 2-4" (10cm)
Minimum Tank Size: 10 Gallons (40 litre)
Water Conditions: 72-82° F, 22-27° C, dH 5-20, pH 6.0-8.0
Diet: Omnivore
Origin: India, West Bengal
Aquarium Type: Community

Notes:
Dwarf Gouramis are appreciative of environments that include dark fine substrates and an abundance of live plants, which accentuate their brilliant colouration. While they thrive best in groups of three or more, they should be kept away from large, aggressive fish. They are, however, compatible with other small, peaceful fish as well as fellow gouramis. As omnivores, these fish enjoy both plant-based and meaty foods. Feed them an algae-based flake food, along with supplemental offerings of freeze-dried bloodworms and tubifex worms. Occasionally, you can also provide fresh or frozen foods for a more balanced diet.

Chapter 8: Labyrinth Fish

Giant Gourami

The Giant Gourami exhibits a pale to golden yellow colouration, decorated with silvery, pale blue stripes running vertically along its body.

Scientific Name: Osphronemus goramy
Care Level: Easy
Temperament: Semi-aggressive
Maximum Size: 24" (60cm)
Minimum Tank Size: 150 Gallons (570 litre)
Water Conditions: 72-82° F, 22-28° C, dH 5-20, pH 6.0-8.0
Diet: Omnivore
Origin: Southeast Asia
Aquarium Type: Semi-aggressive Community

Notes:
Given their potential size, these impressive fish should only be considered for large aquarium setups. They are known to be compatible with other robust fish species such as Silver Dollars, Knife Fish, and Plecos. Their habitat should include elements like live plants, rocks, and driftwood for them to explore and use as hiding spots. Their diet should consist of high-quality pellet food supplemented with a variety of foods like frozen bloodworms, brine shrimp, and fresh vegetables like spinach and lettuce. Occasionally, live foods such as earthworms can be offered for additional nutrition.

Chapter 8: Labyrinth Fish

Paradise Fish

This species exhibits vibrant red and blue markings along its body, contributing to a visually striking appearance.

Scientific Name: Macropodus opercularis
Care Level: Easy
Temperament: Semi-aggressive
Maximum Size: 4" (10cm)
Minimum Tank Size: 20 Gallons (75 litre)
Water Conditions: 64-82° F, 18-28° C, dH 5-20, pH 6.0-8.0
Diet: Omnivore
Origin: East Asia
Aquarium Type: Community, but caution required

Notes:
Paradise Fish are known for their territorial behaviour and therefore require ample space and numerous hiding spots. It's best to house them with similarly sized fish that can hold their own but are not overly aggressive. Keeping multiple male Paradise Fish together is not recommended due to their aggressive territorial behavior, which can escalate to deadly fights, much like their Betta counterparts. Their diet should consist of a good balance between plant-based and meaty foods. An algae-based flake food, supplemented with protein-rich options like freeze-dried bloodworms and tubifex, would meet their nutritional needs.

Chapter 8: Labyrinth Fish

Pearl Gourami

This species has a unique brownish-silver hue, which is highlighted by a pearl-like pattern. A distinctive black line extends from the eye to the tail.

Scientific Name: Trichopodus leerii
Care Level: Easy
Temperament: Peaceful
Maximum Size: 4" (10cm)
Minimum Tank Size: 30 Gallons (115 litre)
Water Conditions: 77-82° F, 25-28° C, dH 4-20, pH 6.0-7.5
Diet: Omnivore
Origin: Southeast Asia
Aquarium Type: Community

Notes:
The Pearl Gourami appreciates environments with dark fine substrates and an abundance of live plants, which can enhance the display of its brilliant colouration. Suitable tank mates include those that are peaceful, not overly large, or excessively active. The Pearl Gourami cohabitates well with other community species such as angelfish, tetras, barbs, danios, and similar species. A varied diet is beneficial for these fish. Incorporate a mix of flake food, crisps, freeze-dried bloodworms, brine shrimp, and frozen foods to meet their nutritional needs.

Chapter 8: Labyrinth Fish

Three Spot Gourami

The Three Spot Gourami is a striking fish recognized for its distinctive appearance. It has is three spots on its body: one spot in the middle, one at the base of the tail, and one that is actually the fish's eye. The colors can vary, but they are often silvery-blue with a hint of gold, and their spots are usually dark.

Scientific Name: Trichopodus trichopterus
Care Level: Easy
Temperament: Peaceful
Maximum Size: 6" (15cm)
Minimum Tank Size: 30 Gallons (115 litre)
Water Conditions: 72-82° F, 22-28° C, dH 4-18, pH 6.0-8.0
Diet: Omnivore
Origin: Southeast Asia
Aquarium Type: Community

Notes:
It's advisable to keep only one male per aquarium, as males of this species can become aggressive with each other. The aquarium should have a good number of hiding places, created with rocks and driftwood, but also maintain ample open swimming space. As this species is known for jumping, a secure tank lid is essential. Their diet should include a mix of tubifex worms, earthworms, glass worms, and brine shrimp, in addition to flake and freeze-dried foods. Complement their diet with spirulina-based foods and lightly cooked vegetables like lettuce, zucchini/courgette, or peas.

Chapter 8: Labyrinth Fish

Golden Gourami

This fish typically displays a bright yellow or gold color, and occasionally a deep orange hue, with subtle light stripes visible along its back.

Scientific Name: Trichopodus trichopterus gold
Care Level: Easy
Temperament: Peaceful, but can exhibit aggression towards smaller fish
Maximum Size: 6" (15cm)
Minimum Tank Size: 30 Gallons (100 litre)
Water Conditions: 74-86° F, 24-30° C, dH 5-18, pH 6.5-8.0
Diet: Omnivore
Origin: Southeast Asia
Aquarium Type: Community

Notes:
The Golden Gourami appreciates a tank with dark, fine substrates and an abundance of live plants, which can accentuate its brilliant golden coloration. Behaviour can vary among individuals, with some remaining peaceful while others may become more aggressive, occasionally targeting smaller fish. Males tend to be territorial and can engage in disputes with each other. Therefore, the most suitable tankmates are other fish of a similar size and temperament. Their diet can include a variety of foods such as flakes, crisps, freeze-dried bloodworms or black worms, brine shrimp, and other frozen foods.

Chapter 8: Labyrinth Fish

Pygmy Sparkling Gourami

These fish shimmer with splashes of red, green, and blue and are known to produce an audible croaking sound using a specialized pectoral mechanism.

Scientific Name: Trichopsis pumila
Care Level: Easy
Temperament: Peaceful
Maximum Size: 1 ½" (4cm)
Minimum Tank Size: 10 Gallons (40 litre)
Water Conditions: 72-78° F, 22-25° C, dH 4-8, pH 6.0-7.0
Diet: Omnivore
Origin: Southeast Asia, especially Cambodia
Aquarium Type: Community

Notes:
These fish flourish best in an aquarium set up with live plants, rocks, or driftwood for them to explore. A dark substrate can enhance the sparkling colouration of these gouramis. They are compatible with a variety of tank mates that are of similar size and share a peaceful temperament. Despite their peaceful nature, they are also quite shy. Therefore, they should not be kept with very boisterous or overly active fish species that could cause them stress. Due to their small size, they can easily be preyed upon by larger fish. Their diet should consist of a mix of flake foods, crisps, freeze-dried bloodworms or black worms, brine shrimp, and frozen foods.

Chapter 8: Labyrinth Fish

Silver/Moonlight Gourami

The silver/moonlight gourami boasts a silver coloration with a slightly greenish hue, reminiscent of soft moonlight.

Scientific Name: Trichopodus microlepis
Care Level: Easy
Temperament: Peaceful
Maximum Size: 6" (15cm)
Minimum Tank Size: 30 Gallons (100 litre)
Water Conditions: 77-86° F, 25-30° C, dH 2-25, pH 6.0-7.5
Diet: Omnivore
Origin: Thailand
Aquarium Type: Community

Notes:
The silver/moonlight gourami benefits from a dark, fine substrate and an abundance of live plants, which help to accentuate its striking colouration. Avoid housing this gourami with smaller fish species, such as neon tetras or shrimp, that could potentially fit in its mouth. Ideal tankmates encompass other Trichogaster, Colisa, Botia, Corydoras, barbs, angelfish, and Loricariids. Be aware that males may exhibit territorial behaviour with other males and gouramis. As omnivores, these fish enjoy a varied diet that can include flake food, frozen brine shrimp, algae flakes, and bloodworms.

Chapter 8: Labyrinth Fish

Kissing Gourami

This unique fish stands out with its characteristic "kissing" behaviour, which makes for an interesting display in any aquarium.

Scientific Name: Helostoma temminckii (Helostomatidae Family)
Care Level: Moderate
Temperament: Semi-aggressive
Maximum Size: 6" (15cm)
Minimum Tank Size: 30 Gallons (100 litre)
Water Conditions: 72-84° F, 22-28° C, dH 5-20, pH 6.0-8.0
Diet: Omnivore
Origin: Southeast Asia
Aquarium Type: Community

Notes:
Kissing gouramis appreciate environments that feature dark, fine substrates and plenty of plants, as these help to enhance their vivid colouration. However, bear in mind that these fish have a habit of nibbling on live plants, so it may be beneficial to use either plastic or very hardy live plants in the tank. Their "kissing" behaviour, which can be directed towards each other, the aquarium floor, or decor, is a captivating sight. When considering tank mates, opt for fish that are peaceful to semi-aggressive in nature. However, very small fish like neon tetras or similar species may be at risk of being eaten by the kissing gouramis. In terms of diet, these gouramis appreciate a varied menu that includes flakes, crisps, freeze-dried blood worms or black worms, brine shrimp, and frozen foods.

Chapter 8: Labyrinth Fish

Siamese "Betta" Fighting Fish

Betta fish, renowned for their vibrant colours and large, flowing fins that come in shades of green, brown, red, and grey, make a visually striking addition to any aquarium.

Scientific Name: Betta splendens
Care Level: Easy
Temperament: Peaceful, but one male should be kept per tank.
Maximum Size: 3" (7cm)
Minimum Tank Size: 10 Gallons (40 litre)
Water Conditions: 75-86° F, 23-30° C, dH 0-20, pH 6.0-8.0
Diet: Carnivore
Origin: Thailand
Aquarium Type: Community

Notes:
While Betta fish are generally peaceful, males are notorious for their aggression towards each other. As such, it is imperative to house only one male per aquarium to prevent lethal fights. Females, on the other hand, may be housed together, albeit with some caution. Betta fish should ideally share their space with other species that won't nip at their large, delicate fins; thus, it's advisable to avoid keeping them with barbs. A well-decorated aquarium with numerous hiding spots amongst freshwater plant foliage is preferred by these fish. As for diet, Betta fish are carnivorous and thrive on quality flake food, frozen or freeze-dried bloodworms, and brine shrimp.

9 Cyprinids

Cyprinids, members of the Cyprinidae family, are an excellent choice for beginner aquarists due to their low-maintenance nature and resilience. They can adapt to a wide range of water conditions, although they typically prefer soft, slightly acidic water.

These fish place a premium on cleanliness, necessitating regular partial water changes to maintain their habitat in optimal conditions. Their preferred water temperature aligns with that of most tropical fish, averaging around 75° F (24°C).

Cyprinids are known for their social behavior and are most comfortable when kept in schools. Observing a group of 20 or more of these fish swimming in unison can make for a truly spectacular display.

Bright lighting and outside distractions generally do not distress them, except during feeding time when they exhibit noticeable excitement. Regular feedings and a clean, comfortable environment will help keep your Cyprinids healthy and content.

Chapter 9: Cyprinids

Black Ruby Barb

The Black Ruby Barb displays a captivating dark ruby red hue, typically accented with black fins that become darker towards the tail.

Scientific Name: Pethia nigrofasciatus
Care Level: Easy
Temperament: Peaceful
Maximum Size: 2.5" (6cm)
Minimum Tank Size: 30 Gallons (113 litre)
Water Conditions: 68-79° F, 20-26° C, dH 8-12, pH 5.5-7.5
Diet: Omnivore
Origin: Indonesia
Aquarium Type: Community

Notes:
These fish exhibit peaceful behavior but are not compatible with species with long fins, such as guppies and bettas. They thrive best when kept in groups of five or more. These barbs are very active swimmers and they need plenty of open swimming space in the tank. Hence, ensure your aquarium has open areas along with planted regions. The optimal setup for Black Ruby Barbs involves dark decor and an abundance of plants, creating the shady retreats these fish appreciate. Be mindful, though, as they tend to nibble on delicate, leafy plants. Their diet should consist of flake food, green flake, spinach, and small frozen foods, such as daphnia. They have a relatively short lifespan, typically around 4-6 years in captivity with good care.

Chapter 9: Cyprinids

Checker Barb

The Checker Barb, also known as Checkerboard Barb, has a distinctive black and silver-green checkered pattern along its body.

Scientific Name: Oliotus oligolepis
Care Level: Easy
Temperament: Peaceful
Maximum Size: 2" (5cm)
Minimum Tank Size: 30 Gallons (100 litre)
Water Conditions: 68-79° F, 20-26° C, dH 8-12, pH 5.5-7.5
Diet: Omnivore
Origin: Indonesia
Aquarium Type: Community

Notes:
These fish are peaceful but should not be kept with long-finned fish such as guppies and bettas. They should be kept in groups of 5 or more for their well-being. These barbs are generally not territorial, which makes them a good choice for a community tank. However, due to their active nature, they could inadvertently stress out more slow-moving or shy species, so potential tank mates should be chosen with this in mind. The aquarium should be arranged with plenty of plants and dark décor to provide appreciated shady hiding areas. Their diet can include flake food, green flake food, spinach, and small frozen foods such as daphnia. Some sources may list the Checker Barb under the scientific name Puntius oligolepis, but this is outdated taxonomy. The correct name is Oliotus oligolepis.

Chapter 9: Cyprinids

Cherry Barb

These little barbs are characterized by their vivid red coloration, often accompanied by a dotted black pattern along their flanks.

Scientific Name: Puntius titteya
Care Level: Easy
Temperament: Peaceful
Maximum Size: 2" (5cm)
Minimum Tank Size: 20 Gallons (75 litre)
Water Conditions: 74-81° F, 23-27° C, dH 4-19, pH 6.0-7.5
Diet: Omnivore
Origin: Sri Lanka
Aquarium Type: Community

Notes:
Cherry Barbs are peaceful fish but should not be housed with species known for fin nipping such as some guppies and bettas. They are shoaling fish and should be kept in groups of at least 5 individuals. The ideal aquarium setup for Cherry Barbs includes dark substrates and plenty of live plants, which provide both shade and hiding spots. Cherry Barbs accept a variety of foods including flake, green flake, spinach, as well as small frozen foods such as daphnia. For optimal health, it's best to offer them a diverse diet. Lastly, it's worth noting that the color of Cherry Barbs can be indicative of their mood and health. Stress, poor health, or suboptimal tank conditions may result in a paler colouration.

Chapter 9: Cyprinids

Clown Barb

The Clown Barb is usually characterized by its silver hue, complemented by black horizontal check marks that adorn the sides of its body.

Scientific Name: Puntius everetti
Care Level: Easy
Temperament: Peaceful
Maximum Size: 6" (15cm)
Minimum Tank Size: 55 Gallons (200 litres)
Water Conditions: 75-85° F, 24-29° C, dH 2-10, pH 6.0-7.0
Diet: Omnivore
Origin: Southeast Asia, specifically Malaysia and Indonesia
Aquarium Type: Community

Notes:
Being an active species, these fish should be accommodated in aquariums that are at least 4ft long. It's recommended to keep them in shoals of 5 or more, and they can coexist peacefully with similar-sized tank mates. They make ideal companions for medium-sized loaches. While Clown Barbs tend to nibble on soft-leaved plants, they prefer environments with dark décor, robust plants, and ample shady areas for hiding. Their diet can consist of flake, green flake, slow-sinking pellet foods, lettuce, spinach, and various frozen foods. The Clown Barb is known to be a relatively hardy fish, and thus, is quite suitable for beginners and those new to fish keeping. However, keep in mind that while this species is generally peaceful, they may display a degree of aggression during feeding times.

Chapter 9: Cyprinids

Flying Fox

This fish usually has an olive brown colouring on its body, contrasted by a dark black line and a gold streak running from its mouth/eye to the tail.

Scientific Name: Epalzeorhynchos kalopterus
Care Level: Easy
Temperament: Generally Peaceful
Maximum Size: 5" (12cm)
Minimum Tank Size: 30 Gallons (120 litres)
Water Conditions: 73-81° F, 22-27° C, dH 5-12, pH 6.0-7.5
Diet: Omnivore
Origin: Southeast Asia
Aquarium Type: Community

Notes:
These fish can be kept individually, but also tolerate being kept in groups. However, keep an eye for any territorial behavior especially if housed with similar species. They are compatible with various fish such as angelfish, barbs, danios, gouramis, knifefish, loaches, tetras, and rasboras. While generally peaceful, the Flying Fox may show aggressive tendencies towards smaller or similar-looking fish, especially when hungry. An aquarium for Flying Foxes should have plenty of broad-leaved plants, rocks, and driftwood to serve as hiding and resting places. Their diet should consist of a mix of high-quality flakes, wafers, and tablets, as well as vegetable matter such as spinach, zucchini, and lettuce. They are also known to eat algae, serving as a natural tank cleaner.

Chapter 9: Cyprinids

Golden Barb

This barb features greenish/yellow markings on its sides, contrasted by a light reddish-brown colouring on its back.

Scientific Name: Barbodes semifasciolatus
Care Level: Easy
Temperament: Peaceful
Maximum Size: 3" (7.5cm)
Minimum Tank Size: 20 Gallons (75 litres)
Water Conditions: 68-79° F, 20-26° C, dH 5-19, pH 6.0-7.0
Diet: Omnivore
Origin: China, Vietnam
Aquarium Type: Community

Notes:
Golden Barbs are peaceful schooling fish that prefer to be kept in groups of at least 5 or more for their social well-being. They should not be kept with aggressive species or those with long fins such as guppies and bettas, which they might nip at. They thrive best when their environment mimics their natural habitat, so add features such as driftwood, river rocks, and plenty of hiding places to help create a more comfortable home for them. Keep in mind that they have a tendency to nibble on fine-leaved plants. Golden Barbs will appreciate a varied diet that includes a good quality flake food, green flakes, spinach, and small frozen foods such as daphnia. Also, consider providing live foods occasionally for optimal health. Golden Barbs are quite adaptable and resilient, making them an excellent choice for beginner aquarists.

Chapter 9: Cyprinids

Odessa Barb & One-spot Barb

The Odessa Barb, also known as the One-spot Barb, is typically characterized by bright red coloring on its sides with a beige to light brown body.

Scientific Name: Pethia padamya
Care Level: Easy
Temperament: Peaceful
Maximum Size: 3" (7cm)
Minimum Tank Size: 20 Gallons (75 litres)
Water Conditions: 72-82° F, 22-28° C, dH 6-16, pH 6.0-7.5
Diet: Omnivore
Origin: Myanmar, Southeast Asia
Aquarium Type: Community

Notes:
These fish are generally peaceful but should not be kept with long-finned species such as guppies and bettas due to the risk of nipping. They are a schooling fish and should be kept in groups of 5 or more to promote social behavior and reduce stress. The aquarium should be set up with dark décor and an abundance of plant life to provide the shady hiding spots that these fish appreciate. However, note that they have a tendency to nibble on fine-leaved plants. Feeding them a varied diet of quality flake food, green flakes, spinach, and small frozen foods such as daphnia will help to keep them healthy and vibrant.

Chapter 9: Cyprinids

Red Line Torpedo Barb

The Red Line Torpedo Barb, characterized by its silver scales, torpedo-shaped body, distinctive black stripe along its side, and red markings over the eye, is a vibrant addition to any aquarium.

Scientific Name: Sahyadria denisonii
Care Level: Intermediate
Temperament: Peaceful
Maximum Size: 6" (15cm)
Minimum Tank Size: 55 Gallons (210 litres)
Water Conditions: 64-77° F, 18-25° C, dH 5-20, pH 6.5-7.8
Diet: Omnivore
Origin: India
Aquarium Type: Specialist Community

Notes:
These fish are active swimmers and require a spacious aquarium, ideally 4ft long. It is recommended to keep them in shoals of 6 or more to encourage natural schooling behaviour and stress reduction. They make great companions for other medium-sized fish such as loaches, rainbowfish species, other barbs, or larger danios. While they might nibble on soft-leaved plants, the presence of robust plants is beneficial for providing them with much-appreciated shady hiding areas. A dark-themed décor can help to accentuate their colors. Their diet should be varied, including quality flake food, green flakes, slow-sinking pellet foods, and fresh vegetables such as lettuce and spinach. Additionally, they can be fed frozen foods as a treat.

Chapter 9: Cyprinids

Tiger Barb

The Tiger Barb, known for its distinctive silver/light brown coloration with dark vertical black stripes along the side of its body, makes a striking addition to an aquarium.

Scientific Name: Puntigrus tetrazona
Care Level: Easy
Temperament: Semi-aggressive
Maximum Size: 3" (7cm)
Minimum Tank Size: 30 Gallons (115 litre)
Water Conditions: 70-79° F, 21-26° C, dH 10-15, pH 6.0-7.0
Diet: Omnivore
Origin: Southeast Asia
Aquarium Type: Community

Notes:
While these fish are generally peaceful, they can become semi-aggressive if not kept in adequate numbers or with inappropriate tank mates. It's recommended to keep them in schools of 8 or more to disperse aggression and limit fin-nipping behavior. Tiger Barbs are not recommended for tanks with long-finned fish such as guppies and bettas, as they might nip at their fins. The aquarium should be set up with a variety of hiding spaces, including plenty of plants and dark décor, to provide these fish with comfort and security. In terms of diet, Tiger Barbs thrive on a varied diet that includes good quality flake food, green flake, micropellets, slow-sinking pellets (for larger specimens), and frozen foods for nutritional diversity.

Chapter 9: Cyprinids

Tinfoil Barb

The Tinfoil Barb, known for its brilliant silver hue with distinct red markings on its tail and pectoral fins, is a large and lively addition to an aquarium.

Scientific Name: Barbonymus schwanenfeldii
Care Level: Easy
Temperament: Peaceful
Maximum Size: 14" (35cm)
Minimum Tank Size: 75 Gallons (280 litres)
Water Conditions: 72-77° F, 22-25° C, dH 4-20, pH 6.0-7.5
Diet: Omnivore
Origin: Southeast Asia
Aquarium Type: Community

Notes:

Tinfoil Barbs are peaceful, gregarious fish that are best kept in groups of 5 or more. They coexist well with other medium to large-sized fish of similar temperament. However, keep in mind that these robust barbs can easily consume smaller fish, so tankmates should be chosen with care. As these fish are known to jump, ensure your aquarium has a secure cover to prevent escapes. An adult Tinfoil Barb can be quite heavy, making their leaps potentially dangerous for both the fish and the aquarium. The aquarium should be spacious and feature dark décor and robust, hardy plants to provide the fish with appreciated hiding areas. Given their propensity to nibble on aquatic plants, select plant species that can withstand this behavior. Tinfoil Barbs thrive on a varied diet of flake food, small sinking pellets, and small frozen foods such as mosquito larvae, brine shrimp, and daphnia. As the fish grow larger, they can be offered larger frozen foods such as krill, Mysis shrimp, and chopped prawns or cockle.

Chapter 9: Cyprinids

Bala Shark

The Bala Shark, also known as the Silver Shark or Shark Minnow, is known for its vibrant silver body and distinctive black markings on its fins.

Scientific Name: Balantiocheilos melanopterus
Care Level: Moderate
Temperament: Peaceful
Maximum Size: 14" (35cm)
Minimum Tank Size: 150 Gallons (570 litres)
Water Conditions: 72-82° F, 22-28° C, dH 10-13, pH 6.0-7.5
Diet: Omnivore
Origin: Southeast Asia
Aquarium Type: Specialist Community

Notes:
Bala Sharks are social creatures and do best in groups of at least 5 or 6. They require ample swimming space, so they are best suited to large, well-filtered aquariums. Tanks should be planted at the sides and back to allow a spacious central swimming area. They are generally peaceful but may be startled easily, darting quickly which can lead to potential injury. Therefore, choose your aquarium decor with caution to avoid any sharp or potentially harmful items. Bala Sharks coexist well with other peaceful, similarly-sized fish, but aggressive species should be avoided as tankmates. Feeding them a diverse diet of flake food, slow-sinking pellets, and frozen foods like mosquito larvae, brine shrimp, and Mysis shrimp will ensure their nutritional needs are met. Larger specimens may also enjoy krill.

Chapter 9: Cyprinids

Red-Tailed Black Shark

The Red-Tailed Black Shark, distinct for its deep black body and vibrant red tail, is a fascinating aquarium inhabitant.

Scientific Name: Epalzeorhynchos bicolor
Care Level: Moderate
Temperament: Semi-aggressive, especially as it matures
Maximum Size: 6" (15cm)
Minimum Tank Size: 55 Gallons (210 litres)
Water Conditions: 72-79° F, 22-26° C, dH 10-15, pH 6.5-7.5
Diet: Omnivore
Origin: Thailand
Aquarium Type: Semi-Aggressive Community

Notes:
Red-Tailed Black Sharks are notably territorial and generally do not tolerate the presence of their own species or similar species in the tank. For this reason, it's recommended to house them individually within a community tank. They need a minimum tank length of 4ft with a soft substrate to protect their sensory barbels. The aquarium should include ample hiding places, such as caves, bogwood, and plants. Despite their semi-aggressive nature, these fish can coexist with medium-sized fish that inhabit upper tank levels, such as barbs, danios, rainbow fish, and larger species of tetra. Feeding Red-Tailed Black Sharks a varied diet is key. They will appreciate sinking catfish pellets, flake food, green flakes, algae wafers, as well as fresh vegetables. Algae growth in the tank will also be appreciated. They will also benefit from occasional servings of frozen foods such as mosquito larvae.

Chapter 9: Cyprinids

Ruby Rainbow Shark

The Ruby Rainbow Shark, sharing similar characteristics with the Red-Tailed Black Shark, is usually black in color with distinctive red or orange fins.

Scientific Name: Epalzeorhynchos frenatum
Care Level: Moderate
Temperament: Generally peaceful, but can become aggressive as they age
Maximum Size: 6" (15cm)
Minimum Tank Size: 55 Gallons (210 litres)
Water Conditions: 72-79° F, 22-26° C, dH 10-15, pH 6.5-7.5
Diet: Omnivore
Origin: Thailand
Aquarium Type: Semi-Aggressive Community

Notes:
Ruby Rainbow Sharks are characteristically territorial and should ideally be kept singly to avoid conflicts with similar species. The aquarium should be spacious, with a minimum length of 4ft, and feature a soft substrate to safeguard the delicate sensory barbels of these fish. The tank should also include a variety of hiding places such as rocky caves, driftwood, and live plants. Despite their territorial behaviour, these fish can cohabit with medium-sized species like barbs, danios, rainbow fish, and larger tetra species, provided these other species predominantly occupy the upper levels of the tank. Feeding Ruby Rainbow Sharks involves a mix of sinking catfish pellets, flake food, green flake, algae wafers, along with naturally occurring algae in the tank. Including vegetable matter and occasional servings of frozen foods like mosquito larvae is beneficial to their diet.

Chapter 9: Cyprinids

Siamese Algae Eater

The Siamese Algae Eater, typically silver in color, features a long black stripe extending across the center of its body.

Scientific Name: Crossocheilus oblongus
Care Level: Easy
Temperament: Generally Peaceful
Maximum Size: 6" (15cm)
Minimum Tank Size: 30 Gallons (114 litres)
Water Conditions: 75-79° F, 24-26° C, dH 5-20, pH 6.5-7.0
Diet: Omnivore, but primarily herbivorous
Origin: Southeast Asia
Aquarium Type: Community

Notes:
Siamese Algae Eaters are great companions for various species such as barbs, rasboras, loaches, rainbowfish, and some larger tetra species. However, it's advisable to avoid housing them with closely related or similar-looking species to prevent aggression. An aquarium environment enriched with hiding spots, including rocky caves, driftwood, and live plants, will be highly beneficial for these fish. Feeding Siamese Algae Eaters should include a variety of sinking catfish pellets, algae wafers, and small frozen foods. Supplementing their diet with vegetable matter such as cucumber and spinach is beneficial. They are renowned for their ability to consume several types of algae, effectively browsing the tank surfaces for these.

Chapter 9: Cyprinids

Harlequin Rasbora

This fish typically has an orange-red body with a distinctive black marking towards its back, reminiscent of a pork chop shape.

Scientific Name: Trigonostigma heteromorpha
Care Level: Easy
Temperament: Peaceful
Maximum Size: 2" (5cm)
Minimum Tank Size: 10 Gallons (38 litre)
Water Conditions: 74-82° F, 22-28° C, dH 6-10, pH 5.0-7.5
Diet: Omnivore
Origin: Southeast Asia
Aquarium Type: Community

Notes:
Often nicknamed "pork chop", these fish make a spectacular display when kept in groups of 10 or more. They are a peaceful species, making them ideal for community tanks. However, care should be taken to avoid housing them with large, aggressive species, as they can become stressed or preyed upon. Harlequin Rasboras prefer slightly acidic water, replicating their natural habitat in the peat swamps of Southeast Asia. Regular water changes and monitoring of pH levels can help ensure their environment is suitable. A tank with hiding places amongst rocky caves, bogwood, and live plants will be appreciated. Feeding should consist of a diet of high-quality flakes, micro pellets, and small frozen or live foods such as mosquito larvae, brineshrimp, and daphnia.

10 Danios

Danios, belonging to the Cyprinidae family, originate from the freshwater streams of Southeast Asia. Renowned for their hardiness, they can withstand a diverse range of tank conditions, rendering them an ideal choice for novice aquarists. Many species showcase vibrant colorations and, as active schooling fish, they create stunning visual displays when housed in substantial groups.

These quick and agile swimmers usually prefer the upper and middle levels of the aquarium. They thrive best in tanks with ample swimming space and moderate water flow, replicating their natural riverine habitats.

Danios are peaceful and get along well with many other community fish. They can cohabitate harmoniously with other species that match their active temperament and are not aggressive.

Lastly, with their bright colors, active nature, and ease of care, Danios can add an interesting dynamic to your freshwater aquarium. However, they are also known for their playful jumping behavior, so a tightly fitting lid is recommended for their tank.

Chapter 10: Danios

Giant Danio

The Giant Danio exhibits a vibrant interplay of blue and yellow markings along the sides of its body, complemented by greyish, transparent fins.

Scientific Name: Devario aequipinnatus
Care Level: Easy
Temperament: Semi-Aggressive
Maximum Size: 4" (10cm)
Minimum Tank Size: 30 Gallons (115 litre)
Water Conditions: 72-78° F, 22-25° C, dH 2-20, pH 6.0-8.0
Diet: Omnivore
Origin: Sri Lanka, Nepal, and the West coast of India
Aquarium Type: Community

Notes:
Giant Danios appreciate a well-decorated tank with ample plant cover, driftwood, rocks, and other retreat spaces, yet they need ample open space for swimming. In choosing tank mates, it's essential to pick other semi-aggressive species of a similar size, as these fish can exhibit dominance. Giant Danios are schooling fish in nature and should be kept in groups of at least six for their social wellbeing. Feed them a balanced diet including flake foods, freeze-dried foods, and live foods like blood worms, tubifex worms, and brine shrimp. Also consider offering them occasional servings of frozen foods for nutritional variety. Giant Danios are robust and hardy, making them suitable for beginner aquarists. Despite their semi-aggressive nature, they are largely non-territorial and prefer the upper levels of the aquarium, making them a dynamic addition to a mixed-species tank.

Chapter 10: Danios

Pearl Danio

This danio usually has brownish/yellow, pink/silver body and two light yellow/white or blue/red stripes along its side.

Scientific Name: Danio albolineatus
Care Level: Easy
Temperament: Peaceful
Maximum Size: 2.5" (6cm)
Minimum Tank Size: 10 Gallons (40 litres)
Water Conditions: 64-78° F, 17-25° C, dH 8-12, pH 6.0-7.8
Diet: Omnivore
Origin: Myanmar
Aquarium Type: Community

Notes:
Pearl Danios thrive in an environment that mimics their natural habitat, featuring an array of plants, driftwood, and rocks which provide them with places to hide and retreat. These danios are social, peaceful fish that fare best in the company of other non-aggressive species that are not large enough to consume them. They are schooling fish by nature and prefer to be kept in groups of at least 8. You might see them playfully chasing each other, which is a part of their natural behavior and should not be a cause for concern. Their diet should be balanced and varied, incorporating flake foods, freeze-dried foods, and small live or frozen foods such as blood worms, tubifex worms, and brine shrimp. Despite being omnivores, Pearl Danios have a leaning towards plant matter in their diet. Therefore, along with regular omnivorous fish food, it would be beneficial to occasionally include some vegetables or plant-based flake food.

Chapter 10: Danios

Glowlight Danio

This fish is characterized by orange bands and a series of vertical blue-black stripes along its sides.

Scientific Name: Danio choprai
Care Level: Easy
Temperament: Peaceful
Maximum Size: 1.2" (3cm)
Minimum Tank Size: 20 Gallons (75 litres)
Water Conditions: 72-79°F, 22-26° C, dH 2-10, pH 6.0-7.0
Diet: Omnivore
Origin: Myanmar
Aquarium Type: Community

Notes:
Glowlight Danios appreciate a well-structured environment with plenty of plants, driftwood, rocks, and other hiding places. They are also known to be proficient jumpers, so a secure tank lid is highly recommended to prevent escapes. The ideal tank mates for Glowlight Danios are other peaceful fish species that are not large enough to prey on them. In nature, these danios exhibit shoaling behavior, so they should be kept in groups of at least six individuals. They have a versatile diet that includes flake foods, freeze-dried foods, blood worms, tubifex worms, brine shrimp, as well as some frozen foods. Feeding should be done in small amounts several times a day to avoid overfeeding and to maintain optimal water quality. The water in their tank should be well-oxygenated with a moderate to high flow, replicating their native fast-flowing river habitats. Also, regular water changes are crucial to ensure their health and well-being.

Chapter 10: Danios

Zebra Danio

This fish is characterized by its series of blue and silver/gold stripes running along the length of its body.

Scientific Name: Danio rerio
Care Level: Easy
Temperament: Peaceful
Maximum Size: 2.5" (6cm)
Minimum Tank Size: 10 Gallons (40 litre)
Water Conditions: 64-74° F, 18-24° C, dH 5-19, pH 6.5-7.2
Diet: Omnivore
Origin: Eastern India
Aquarium Type: Community

Notes:
Zebra Danios appreciate a well-planted tank with ample hiding spots, which can be provided with elements such as driftwood, rocks, and aquatic plants. Despite their peaceful nature, they are active swimmers and appreciate having ample space to swim. Ideal tank mates include other peaceful to semi-aggressive species that aren't large enough to pose a predatory threat. Being shoaling fish, Zebra Danios thrive in groups and it's recommended to keep them in schools of 6 or more for their social well-being. Their diet should include a mix of flake foods, freeze-dried foods, and small live foods such as blood worms, tubifex worms, and brine shrimp. Supplementing their diet with occasional servings of vegetable matter and frozen foods can ensure a balanced diet.

Chapter 10: Danios

Glofish Danio

Glofish danios are genetically enhanced for vibrant coloration and are available in shades of neon red, orange, blue, green, and purple. These fish are not artificially dyed.

Scientific Name: Danio rerio
Care Level: Easy
Temperament: Peaceful
Maximum Size: 2.5" (6cm)
Minimum Tank Size: 10 Gallons (40 litre)
Water Conditions: 64-82° F, 18-28° C, dH 2-20, pH 6.5-7.5
Diet: Omnivore
Origin: Laboratory-bred (origin species from Southeast Asia)
Aquarium Type: Community

Notes:
These fish possess luminescent colors and glow when illuminated by specific aquarium lights. They create a visually impressive display when kept in groups of 10 or more. Ideal tank mates should include other peaceful to semi-aggressive fish species that are not large enough to predate on the danios. Glofish Danios will benefit from a diet that includes flake foods, freeze-dried foods, blood worms, tubifex worms, brine shrimp, along with some frozen foods. Provide a balanced diet to ensure optimal color vibrancy and overall health. GloFish are not injected or dyed. They inherit their color directly from their parents, and they maintain the color throughout their lifespan. GloFish Danio prefer a planted tank, with moderate lighting. Dark substrate can help their colors pop and be more vibrant.

11 Angels & Cichlids

Cichlids, pronounced "sick-lid", are members of the Cichlidae family. Boasting over a thousand species, the majority of cichlids originate from the Rift Lakes of Malawi, Tanganyika, and Victoria in Central Africa. These fish are celebrated for their striking colorations, engaging behaviors, and dynamic personalities.

African cichlids are known for their aggression and territoriality, but with the right aquarium setup and an appropriate mix of species, they can coexist and flourish within an aquarium environment.

New World Cichlids, also known as South American Cichlids, are typically hardy and hail from regions of the Amazon River.

The Angelfish is a particularly popular species of New World Cichlid that originates from the Amazon basin. Angelfish can grow to approximately six inches in length and eight inches in height. Their unique body and fin shapes add visual interest and diversity to community aquariums. It's recommended to have a deep tank that provides the Angelfish ample room to swim comfortably with its fins fully extended.

Chapter 11: Angels & Cichlids

Altum Angelfish

This angelfish has a silver body adorned with three vertical brownish/red stripes, and reddish/orange black markings on its dorsal fin.

Scientific Name: Pterophyllum altum
Care Level: Moderate
Temperament: Semi-aggressive
Maximum Size: 6" (15cm)
Minimum Tank Size: 55 Gallons (200 litres)
Water Conditions: 75-82° F, 23-28° C, dH 1-5, pH 5.8-6.5
Diet: Omnivore
Origin: Amazon Basin
Aquarium Type: Community

Notes:
Altum Angelfish thrive in tanks abundant with plants and driftwood. They prefer a dimly lit tank with areas of shade provided by plants and decorations. They require a well-maintained aquarium and prefer clean, slightly acidic water with good flow. In groups, these freshwater Angelfish can be territorial, often squabbling until a dominant male is established. They can be kept as individuals, in mated pairs, or in medium-sized groups of 6 or more, but should be paired with other fish species large enough not to be preyed upon. Altum Angelfish readily accept a diet of flake, pellet, and frozen foods.

Chapter 11: Angels & Cichlids

Koi Angelfish

This Angelfish displays a predominantly white body with distinctive black markings and a vibrant orange splash on its head.

Scientific Name: Pterophyllum scalare
Care Level: Moderate
Temperament: Semi-aggressive
Maximum Size: 6" (15cm)
Minimum Tank Size: 55 Gallons (200 litre)
Water Conditions: 75-82° F, 23-27° C, dH 1-5, pH 6.0-7.0
Diet: Omnivore
Origin: Amazon
Aquarium Type: Community

Notes:
Koi Angelfish thrive in tanks with ample plants and driftwood to simulate their natural habitat. Angelfish are territorial creatures and groups will establish a hierarchy through occasional displays of dominance. These fish can be kept individually, as mated pairs, or in moderate-sized groups of six or more. Their tankmates should be other fish species large enough to avoid becoming their prey. Koi Angelfish are not fussy eaters and will readily consume a variety of foods including flake, pellet, and frozen offerings. Koi Angelfish are also known for their graceful swimming, which is an attractive quality that adds to the appeal of your aquarium. However, their long, flowing fins make them susceptible to fin-nipping from aggressive tank mates, so be cautious when choosing companions for your Angelfish.

Chapter 11: Angels & Cichlids

Gold Angelfish

This Angelfish is predominantly silver with golden markings on its head and dorsal fin.

Scientific Name: Pterophyllum scalare
Care Level: Moderate
Temperament: Semi-aggressive
Maximum Size: 6" (15cm)
Minimum Tank Size: 55 Gallons (200 litre)
Water Conditions: 75-82° F, 23-27° C, dH 1-5, pH 6.0-7.0
Diet: Omnivore
Origin: Amazon
Aquarium Type: Community

Notes:
Gold Angelfish thrive in tanks with an abundance of plants and driftwood for cover. Freshwater Angelfish, as a species, are territorial; a group of these fish will establish a hierarchy, often with a dominant male at the top. They can be kept individually, in mated pairs, or in medium-sized groups of 6 or more. Care should be taken when choosing tank mates, as these fish can be semi-aggressive and should be housed with other species that are not small enough to be considered prey. Gold Angelfish readily accept a variety of foods, including flake, pellet, and frozen varieties.

Chapter 11: Angels & Cichlids

Green Terror Cichlid

This cichlid showcases a greenish-white hue with distinct blue spots located beneath its mouth.

Scientific Name: Andinoacara rivulatus
Care Level: Moderate
Temperament: Aggressive
Maximum Size: 12" (30cm)
Minimum Tank Size: 75 Gallons (300 litre)
Water Conditions: 73-79° F, 22-26° C, dH 10-20, pH 6.5-8.0
Diet: Omnivore
Origin: South America
Aquarium Type: Cichlid-American

Notes:
Green Terror Cichlids have an assertive temperament and are best housed with other robust and similar-tempered fish, including certain cichlid species. Tankmates could include other robust cichlids, large catfish, or large characins. However, always monitor interactions to ensure compatibility. Regular water changes are essential. Green Terror Cichlids are sensitive to poor water conditions, which can result in health issues. For a balanced diet, offer them a mix of foods such as cichlid pellets, flakes, bloodworms, and shrimp. A sandy substrate can be beneficial for Green Terror Cichlids, as they sometimes like to sift through it and can also dig around creating their preferred layout. Incorporate rocks, caves, and driftwood to provide hiding spaces and to establish territories.

Chapter 11: Angels & Cichlids

Oscar

Oscars are highly popular due to their distinctive personalities. They can be both entertaining and playful, often forming a bond with their owners.

Scientific Name: Astronotus ocellatus
Care Level: Moderate
Temperament: Despite their size, they are generally peaceful but can be territorial.
Maximum Size: 12" (30cm)
Minimum Tank Size: 75 Gallons (300 litre)
Water Conditions: 73-79° F, 22-26° C, dH 5-20, pH 6.5-8.0
Diet: Carnivore
Origin: South America
Aquarium Type: Cichlid-American

Notes:
It is essential not to house Oscars with fish small enough to be considered prey. They are best paired with similarly sized fish to avoid predatory behavior. Oscars have a tendency to re-arrange their environment. Ensure that your tank setup includes decor without sharp edges and that all equipment, such as filters and heaters, is securely fixed and well-protected. Providing a substrate, like sand or gravel, allows them to engage in their natural digging behavior. Their diet should consist of meaty foods. They are particularly fond of earthworms. For variety and enrichment, consider occasionally offering live insects, such as crickets, which can be sourced from most pet stores.

Chapter 11: Angels & Cichlids

Rams

Rams are vibrantly colored with shades of gold, yellow, blue, and black. They also boast a striking red patch on their abdomen.

Scientific Name: Mikrogeophagus ramirezi
Care Level: Advanced
Temperament: Generally peaceful
Maximum Size: 3" (7cm)
Minimum Tank Size: 20 Gallons (80 litre)
Water Conditions: 72-80° F, 22-26° C, dH 5-10, pH 5.0-7.0
Diet: Omnivore
Origin: South America
Aquarium Type: Cichlid-American

Notes:
For optimal social dynamics, it's advisable to keep Rams in groups of 5 or more. Although they're typically peaceful towards other fish species, Rams can display territorial disputes amongst themselves to establish hierarchy within their group. Avoid placing them with very aggressive fish. Suitable tank mates might include small to medium-sized tetras, Corydoras catfish, and other peaceful bottom dwellers. These fish thrive best in aquarium environments that mimic their natural habitats. This includes substrates like sand or gravel, ample plant life, and driftwood to provide shelter. Their dietary needs can be met with a varied diet that includes meaty flakes, mini-pellets, freeze-dried worms, and frozen offerings like brine and shrimp. Rams are known to be sensitive to water parameters. Regular water changes and a well-maintained tank are crucial for their well-being.

Chapter 11: Angels & Cichlids

Convict Cichlid

This cichlid is easily recognizable by its elongated body adorned with black and white vertical stripes.

Scientific Name: Amatitlania nigrofasciata
Care Level: Moderate
Temperament: Territorial
Maximum Size: 6" (15cm)
Minimum Tank Size: 30 Gallons (115 litre)
Water Conditions: 68-79° F, 20-26° C, dH 6-20, pH 6.5-8.0
Diet: Omnivore
Origin: Central America
Aquarium Type: Cichlid-American

Notes:
These cichlids are known to dig, so choose sturdy plants that can tolerate being uprooted or go for artificial plants. Smooth rocks and caves will be appreciated, especially during breeding. While they can coexist with other cichlid species, it's best to house them with fish of similar size and temperament such as large plecos and sharks. Their dietary needs are versatile. They readily accept a wide variety of foods, including flake, frozen, freeze-dried, live foods, and cichlid-specific pellets. Besides the standard black and white-striped variety, there are also pink or albino variants available in the pet trade. Regular water changes are crucial as convict cichlids thrive in clean water. They aren't particularly sensitive to minor water fluctuations, but consistent poor water quality can lead to health issues.

Chapter 11: Angels & Cichlids

Jack Dempsey Cichlid

This cichlid, inspired by its namesake, the renowned boxer Jack Dempsey, boasts a dark brown hue complemented by shimmering green and blue iridescent spots gracing its sides.

Scientific Name: Rocio octofasciata
Care Level: Moderate
Temperament: Aggressive
Maximum Size: 10" (25cm)
Minimum Tank Size: 55 Gallons (200 litre)
Water Conditions: 78-82° F, 25-28° C, dH 5-12, pH 6.5-7.5
Diet: Primarily Carnivorous
Origin: Central America
Aquarium Type: Cichlid-American

Notes:
Jack Dempsey Cichlids are best suited to be housed with other robust and similarly-sized cichlid species due to their aggressive nature. Avoid pairing with peaceful or smaller fish, as they can become territorial and may consume fish that fit into their mouths. Opt for an aquarium substrate like fine sand and ensure a landscape rich in rocks and hiding spots. This not only replicates their natural environment but also provides necessary territories. Although they have a penchant for digging, if you wish to include plants, choose robust and sturdy varieties like Anubias or Java Fern, which can be anchored to rocks or driftwood. Their diet predominantly consists of meaty foods. Offer a diverse menu of cichlid pellets, high-quality flakes, bloodworms, brine shrimp, and occasionally small fish or live foods for optimum health and coloration.

Chapter 11: Angels & Cichlids

Bumblebee Cichlid

Sporting a slender frame, this cichlid showcases bold vertical stripes in contrasting hues of yellow and black, reminiscent of a bumblebee.

Scientific Name: Pseudotropheus crabro
Care Level: Moderate
Temperament: Aggressive
Maximum Size: 8" (20cm)
Minimum Tank Size: 75 Gallons (300 litre)
Water Conditions: 75-82° F, 24-28° C, dH 10-15, pH 7.8-8.5
Diet: Omnivore
Origin: Lake Malawi
Aquarium Type: Cichlid-African

Notes:
Given their aggressive nature, it's recommended to keep Bumblebee Cichlids in a species-specific tank or, alternatively, with other compatible cichlids from Lake Malawi. Although they can coexist with other African cichlids, housing them with more peaceful species may lead to unwanted confrontations. The aquatic environment should ideally mirror their natural habitat in Lake Malawi, rich with rocks and caves for hiding and establishing territories. A varied diet ensures their optimal health and vivid coloration. Incorporate a mix of cichlid pellets, flakes, bloodworms, and occasional shrimp into their feeding routine. High-quality cichlid-specific foods, like cichlid sticks, are particularly recommended.

Chapter 11: Angels & Cichlids

Blue Dolphin Cichlid

Boasting an elongated body and a distinctive cranial hump, this cichlid captivates with a shimmering blend of deep and light blue hues gracing its flanks.

Scientific Name: Cyrtocara moorii
Care Level: Moderate
Temperament: Semi-Aggressive
Maximum Size: 10" (25cm)
Minimum Tank Size: 75 Gallons (300 litre)
Water Conditions: 75-82° F, 24-28° C, dH 10-15, pH 7.8-8.5
Diet: Omnivore
Origin: Lake Malawi
Aquarium Type: Cichlid-African

Notes:
The Blue Dolphin Cichlid thrives best when housed in a species-specific setup or alongside compatible cichlids from Lake Malawi. Owing to their semi-aggressive nature, it's advisable to pair them with fish of similar size and temperament. They may not coexist peacefully in general community tanks. Their ideal habitat should be rich in hiding spots and territories, achieved by adding rocks and caves. While they love to burrow, this behavior can lead to uprooted plants so opt for hardy or artificial plants. The presence of fine sand can also replicate their natural habitat, allowing them to display natural behaviors. To ensure vibrant colors and good health, offer them a balanced diet consisting of cichlid pellets, flakes, bloodworms, and occasional shrimp. Prioritize high-quality cichlid-specific foods, such as cichlid sticks.

Chapter 11: Angels & Cichlids

Kribensis Cichlid

This cichlid boasts an elongated body, adorned with black and yellow stripes along its sides and complemented by a vibrant, fiery red belly.

Scientific Name: Pelvicachromis pulcher
Care Level: Easy
Temperament: Semi-Aggressive
Maximum Size: 4" (10cm)
Minimum Tank Size: 30 Gallons (115 litre)
Water Conditions: 72-82° F, 22-27° C, dH 5-10, pH 6.5-8.5
Diet: Omnivore
Origin: Nigeria
Aquarium Type: Cichlid-African

Notes:
Offer them an environment rich in rocks and caves, complemented with a sandy substrate. They're natural burrowers and will appreciate spaces they can dig into. Kribensis can be territorial, especially during breeding. It's crucial to exercise caution when integrating them into community tanks. They go well with other West African dwarf cichlids, large corydoras or loaches. Avoid fish that are too small, as they might become targets, especially during the Kribensis breeding season. They're also known to nip at the fins of some species, so avoid bettas, guppies, and angels. Provide a diverse diet that includes cichlid pellets, bloodworms, and other appropriate foods. A quality pellet food designed specifically for cichlids (e.g., cichlid sticks) should be a staple in their diet.

12 Discus

Discus Fish are members of the Cichlidae family and are native to the Amazon River basin. They are known for their timid and gentle nature, making them best suited for tanks with their own kind.

While they can come with a higher price tag and grow to a substantial size, they are an impressive sight in large aquariums due to their vibrant colors and graceful movements.

These fish demand an advanced level of care, primarily because of their specific feeding and water quality needs. They thrive in clean, soft, slightly acidic water and necessitate frequent water changes—about 25% weekly—to mitigate toxins.

While they're best kept with their own kind, if you wish to introduce other species, ensure they are non-aggressive and can thrive in similar water conditions. Cardinal tetras, rummy-nose tetras, and dwarf cichlids can be considered as potential tankmates.

They're known to be observant and can recognize their owners. Over time, with gentle interaction, they may become more comfortable and approach the front of the tank when they see familiar faces.

Chapter 12: Discus

Common Discus

The Common Discus stands out with its distinct disc-shaped body, adorned in bright and often intricate patterns of green, red, brown, and blue.

Scientific Name: Symphysodon aequifasciatus
Care Level: Advanced
Temperament: Peaceful
Maximum Size: 8" (20cm)
Minimum Tank Size: 55 Gallons (200 litre)
Water Conditions: 78-86° F (25-30° C), dH 1-3, pH 6.0-7.5
Diet: Carnivore (primarily, but will consume some plant-based foods)
Origin: Amazon, South America
Aquarium Type: Community

Notes:
Discus fish are sensitive to water fluctuations and demand consistent water parameters, especially regarding pH, temperature, and hardness. There is little margin for error, making water quality paramount for their health. They thrive in well-decorated tanks featuring live plants, rocks, and other forms of cover. However, ensure there is ample swimming space. Discus are generally compatible with most tetra species, loaches, cory catfish, smaller plecos, Siamese algae eaters, peaceful rasbora species, rainbowfish, hatchetfish, and pencilfish. Always monitor new introductions closely to ensure harmony. Feed them a varied diet rich in protein. This includes white worms, bloodworms, Tubifex worms, and high-quality pellet or flake foods. While they mainly consume meaty foods, they might nibble on some plant-based items occasionally. Regularly offering vitamin-enriched foods can enhance their vibrant colors.

Chapter 12: Discus

Royal Red Discus

The Royal Red Discus boasts a captivating disc-shaped body. Their radiant red hue contrasts beautifully with the black markings on their tail fin, making them a centerpiece in any aquarium.

Scientific Name: Symphysodon aequifasciatus
Care Level: Advanced
Temperament: Peaceful
Maximum Size: 8" (20cm)
Minimum Tank Size: 55 Gallons (200 litre)
Water Conditions: 79-86° F (25-30° C), dH 1-3, pH 6.0-7.5
Diet: Primarily Carnivore (with occasional plant-based intake)
Origin: Amazon, South America
Aquarium Type: Community

Notes

Royal Red Discus thrive in tanks adorned with abundant live plants, rocks, and other hiding spots. However, ensuring there's enough open swimming space is crucial for their well-being. They are harmonious with most tetra species, loaches, cory catfish, smaller plecos, Siamese algae eaters, peaceful rasbora species, rainbowfish, hatchetfish, and pencilfish. It's vital to monitor new introductions to ensure compatibility. Their diet should consist of freeze-dried bloodworms, tubifex, Discus-specific pellets, high-quality flake food, and other meaty frozen foods. Occasionally, they might show interest in some plant-based foods. Offering vitamin-enriched foods can help maintain their vivid coloration.

Chapter 12: Discus

Red Checkerboard Discus

The Red Checkerboard Discus showcases a luminous blend of white, red, and orange markings, adding a splash of color and elegance to aquariums.

Scientific Name: Symphysodon aequifasciatus
Care Level: Advanced
Temperament: Peaceful
Maximum Size: 8" (20cm)
Minimum Tank Size: 55 Gallons (200 litre)
Water Conditions: 79-86° F (25-30° C), dH 1-3, pH 6.0-7.5
Diet: Primarily Carnivore (with occasional plant-based intake)
Origin: Amazon, South America
Aquarium Type: Community

Notes
Red Checkerboard Discus are most comfortable in well-planted tanks with adequate hiding spots made up of rocks and other structures. Despite this, they still need ample open swimming space. They gel well with most tetra species, loaches, cory catfish, smaller plecos, Siamese algae eaters, peaceful rasbora species, rainbowfish, hatchetfish, and pencilfish. Close observation is recommended when introducing new fish to ensure a peaceful coexistence. Their primary diet consists of freeze-dried bloodworms, tubifex, Discus-specific pellets, high-quality flake food, and meaty frozen foods. Occasionally, they might also appreciate some plant-based foods. Providing them with vitamin-enriched foods will further enhance their striking coloration.

13 Rainbow Fish

Rainbowfish, members of the Melanotaeniidae family, are vibrant freshwater species predominantly found in Australia, New Guinea, and the surrounding islands including those in Cenderawasih Bay and the Raja Ampat Islands.

Often admired for their iridescent colors and slender bodies, rainbowfish display a dazzling array of hues which can change depending on lighting, age, or mood.

Generally peaceful by nature, rainbowfish are schooling fish that prefer to be kept in groups. Their active swimming habits and shimmering colors make them a popular choice for community aquariums.

Rainbowfish thrive in well-oxygenated water with moderate flow. While they are relatively hardy and can adapt to a range of water conditions, maintaining stable parameters, especially pH and temperature, is essential for their well-being.

Given their peaceful temperament, rainbowfish can be paired with a variety of tankmates, including tetras, guppies, and other similarly-sized, non-aggressive fish.

Chapter 13: Rainbow Fish

Red Rainbowfish

These fish are vibrant in a brilliant shade of red, interspersed with hints of orange on their heads and along the dorsal ridge.

Scientific Name: Glossolepis incisus
Care Level: Easy
Temperament: Peaceful
Maximum Size: 5" (12cm)
Minimum Tank Size: 55 Gallons (200 litre)
Water Conditions: 75-82° F, 23-27° C, dH 9-19, pH 7.0-8.0
Diet: Omnivore
Origin: New Guinea
Aquarium Type: Community

Notes:
Ensure a spacious aquarium with abundant plants to cater to their active swimming nature. Given their propensity to leap, it's crucial to have a secure tank cover. As schooling fish, they flourish when kept in groups, preferably of 6 or more. Red Rainbowfish generally get along well with similarly sized fish that have peaceful temperaments. They are often kept with other species of rainbowfish, tetras, rasboras, and other non-aggressive species. Dietary needs include a mix of flake, frozen, and freeze-dried foods, offered 2 to 3 times daily. Red Rainbowfish display brighter colors when they're in good health, have a proper diet, and are kept in optimal water conditions.

Chapter 13: Rainbow Fish

Boeseman's Rainbowfish

This fish showcases a stunning gradient of fiery red with orange and yellow highlights along its tail fin and back, transitioning into a deep indigo blue or purple towards the front.

Scientific Name: Melanotaenia boesemani
Care Level: Easy
Temperament: Peaceful
Maximum Size: 4" (10cm)
Minimum Tank Size: 40 Gallons (150 litre)
Water Conditions: 72-79° F, 22-26° C, dH 9-19, pH 7.0-8.0
Diet: Omnivore
Origin: West Papua, Indonesia
Aquarium Type: Community

Notes:
Boeseman's Rainbowfish thrive in long aquariums with abundant plants, offering plenty of room for these active swimmers. They have a tendency to jump, so it's crucial to have a secure lid on the aquarium. As schooling fish, they flourish when kept in groups of 6 or more. Their peaceable nature makes them compatible with many other non-aggressive species. While they are peaceful and can coexist with many species, it's best to avoid housing them with fin-nippers or overly aggressive fish. Ideal tank mates include other species of rainbowfish, tetras, and small to medium-sized catfish. For their diet, a combination of flake, frozen, and freeze-dried foods, fed 2 to 3 times daily, is optimal. Their best colors typically emerge when they are well-fed and kept in a stress-free environment with proper lighting.

Chapter 13: Rainbow Fish

Neon Rainbowfish

Also known as the dwarf rainbowfish, this species showcases a bright blue body complemented by dashes of red on its fins.

Scientific Name: Melanotaenia praecox
Care Level: Easy
Temperament: Peaceful
Maximum Size: 2.5" (6cm)
Minimum Tank Size: 30 Gallons (113 litres)
Water Conditions: 70-78°F (21-25°C), dH 8-12, pH 6.0-7.5
Diet: Omnivore
Origin: Indonesia
Aquarium Type: Community

Notes:
A spacious and elongated aquarium setup is beneficial for these active swimmers, allowing them plenty of room to glide around. They thrive in the company of their own kind and should ideally be kept in schools of 6 or more. While they are peaceful and get along well with many community tank species, avoid keeping them with larger or aggressive fish that may bully or see them as prey. Neon Rainbowfish prefer a soft substrate, like fine sand, to protect their delicate undersides. Adding driftwood and smooth, water-worn rocks can provide hiding spots and increase their sense of security. Moderate lighting is ideal. While they can tolerate brighter lighting, providing some shaded areas through plants or decor is appreciated. For optimal health and vibrant colors, feed them a mix of flake, frozen, and freeze-dried foods. Aim for 2 to 3 feeding sessions per day.

14 Neotropical Electric Fish

Neo-electric fish, also known as weakly electric fish, are a fascinating group of freshwater fish that possess the unique ability to generate weak electric fields for communication, navigation, and prey detection. They are primarily found in tropical and subtropical regions of South America, Africa, and Asia. This electroreception ability sets them apart from other fish species and makes them a subject of great interest for researchers and aquarium enthusiasts.

Introducing neo-electric fish to a community aquarium with other fish can be challenging and requires careful consideration. Neo-electric fish, such as the Black Ghost Knifefish, Elephant Nose, and other species, have unique behaviors and specific care needs that may not always be compatible with other fish.

Neo-electric fish can grow relatively large, and smaller tankmates may be seen as potential prey. It's essential to choose tankmates that are similar in size or too large to be considered as food.

Keeping neo-electric fish can be more challenging than caring for more common fish. If you are a beginner or new to keeping these unique species, consider gaining experience with other fish species first or seek advice from experienced aquarists.

Chapter 14: Neotropical Electric Fish

Black Ghost Knifefish

Characterized by its deep black body, this fish is adorned with two distinct white rings on its tail and a striking white blaze on its nose and head.

Scientific Name: Apteronotus albifrons
Care Level: Moderate
Temperament: Semi-aggressive
Maximum Size: 12" - 16" (up to 40cm)
Minimum Tank Size: 150 Gallons (500 litres)
Water Conditions: 73-80° F, 22-26° C; dH 0-10; pH 6.5-7.0
Diet: Carnivore
Origin: South America
Aquarium Type: Community

Notes:
The Black Ghost Knifefish thrives in a long aquarium furnished with abundant plants. Opt for fine gravel for substrate and ensure a dimly lit ambiance, reminiscent of their native habitats. Initially, they might exhibit shy and reticent behaviors. However, with patience and time, they can grow more accustomed to their surroundings and even exhibit tameness. Co-habitation with larger species that they don't perceive as prey works best. Their diet primarily consists of live foods, which can range from meats and chopped earthworms to flaked foods. They also consume small fish and frozen foods. Ensure a varied diet for optimal health.

Chapter 14: Neotropical Electric Fish

Zebra Knifefish

Zebra Knifefish have an elongated, eel-like body with a distinctive black and white striped coloration, resembling the stripes of a zebra, hence their common name. They have a long anal fin that runs along the length of their body and a shorter dorsal fin near the tail.

Scientific Name: Gymnotus carapo
Care Level: Moderate
Temperament: Peaceful
Maximum Size: Up to 10" (25 cm)
Minimum Tank Size: 55 gallons (208 liters)
Water Conditions: 75-82°F (24-28°C); dH 2-15; pH 6.5-7.5
Diet: Carnivore
Origin: South America
Aquarium Type: Community

Notes:
Provide hiding spots such as caves, driftwood, and dense vegetation to mimic their natural environment. Zebra Knifefish are primarily nocturnal, so offer subdued lighting to reduce stress. Zebra Knifefish can be kept with other peaceful and non-aggressive fish species. Avoid housing them with smaller fish that may be seen as potential prey. These fish are carnivorous and primarily piscivorous, so their diet should consist of live or frozen foods like brine shrimp, bloodworms, and small fish. Offer a varied diet to ensure proper nutrition.

Chapter 14: Neotropical Electric Fish

Elephant Nose

The Elephant Nose Fish, distinguished by its dark black hue, is aptly named due to its elongated, trunk-like snout. This characteristic is complemented by its uniquely forked tail adorned with a singular white stripe.

Scientific Name: Gnathonemus petersii
Care Level: Advanced
Temperament: Semi-aggressive
Maximum Size: Approximately 9" (25cm)
Minimum Tank Size: 55 Gallons (200 litres)
Water Conditions: 73-80°F (22-27°C); dH 0-10; pH 6.5-7.0
Diet: Carnivore
Origin: Africa
Aquarium Type: Community

Notes:
While generally peaceful, housing them in pairs is discouraged as dominance can lead to the bullying of the weaker fish. They can coexist harmoniously with other docile species such as tetras, angels, and gouramis. These nimble swimmers have a proclivity for leaping, making a secure lid essential for their enclosure. They thrive in tanks with subdued lighting, along with ample hiding spots to offer a sense of security. A delicacy for them includes brine shrimp and bloodworms, whether frozen or live. However, they seldom show interest in flake foods.

15 Gobies

Gobies are a diverse and captivating group of fish known for their intriguing behaviors, striking appearances, and adaptability to various aquatic environments. Belonging to the family Gobiidae, gobies span across freshwater, brackish water, and marine habitats, each showcasing unique characteristics that make them fascinating additions to aquariums.

These fish exhibit a wide range of sizes, from diminutive species barely exceeding an inch in length to larger types that can grow up to a foot long. Gobies possess bodies that are marvels of adaptation, shaped to suit their particular lifestyles. Their elongated forms, enhanced by vibrant colors, intricate patterns, and often adorned with spots or stripes, contribute to their visual allure.

Gobies are known for their varied diets, which can include small crustaceans, insects, worms, and algae. In a home aquarium, it's important to offer a well-rounded diet that consists of high-quality pellets, live or frozen foods, and occasional vegetable matter.

Chapter 15: Gobies

Bumblebee Goby

The Bumblebee Goby boasts a captivating appearance with its distinct black and yellow striped pattern reminiscent of a bumblebee's markings. Its slender, elongated body showcases alternating black and yellow stripes that run from head to tail.

Scientific Name: Brachygobius xanthozonus
Care Level: Moderate
Temperament: Territorial
Maximum Size: Around 1-2 inches (2.5-5 cm)
Minimum Tank Size: 10 gallons (40 litre)
Water Conditions: 74-82°F (23-28°C); dH 2-15; pH 6.5-7.5
Diet: Carnivorous, prefers live or frozen foods like brine shrimp, bloodworms, and small insects
Origin: Southeast Asia
Aquarium Type: Freshwater, species-specific or peaceful community tank with other small, non-aggressive fish

Notes:
Bumblebee Gobies are territorial in nature, especially towards their own kind. Keep them in pairs or small groups to minimize aggression. Provide ample hiding spots like caves and rock formations to alleviate territorial disputes. Create a setup with fine substrate, as Bumblebee Gobies may sift through it in search of food. Add live plants, rocks, and decorations to mimic their natural habitat and provide hiding spots. These gobies are carnivorous and prefer live or frozen foods like brine shrimp, bloodworms, and small insects. Offering a varied diet promotes their health and natural behaviors

Chapter 15: Gobies

Knight Goby

The Knight Goby has a distinctive appearance with a silvery body adorned with black vertical stripes and a notable black spot on the dorsal fin.

Scientific Name: Stigmatogobius sadanundio
Care Level: Moderate
Temperament: Peaceful
Maximum Size: Around 2-3 inches (5-7.5 cm)
Minimum Tank Size: 20 gallons
Water Conditions: 74-82°F (23-28°C); dH 2-15; pH 6.5-7.5
Diet: Omnivorous, prefers a varied diet including high-quality pellets, live or frozen foods, and vegetable matter
Origin: Southeast Asia
Aquarium Type: Freshwater, community tank with other peaceful fish

Notes:
Opt for peaceful community fish like tetras, rasboras, and livebearers that share a similar temperament and won't intimidate or stress the Knight Gobies. Bottom-dwelling species like Kuhli Loaches and Corydoras Catfish can coexist well, utilizing different parts of the tank. Incorporate rock formations, caves, and driftwood to provide hiding spots and create visual barriers. Live plants like Java Fern, Anubias, and floating plants can enhance the aesthetics while offering additional hiding places. Knight Gobies are omnivorous and appreciate a varied diet that includes high-quality pellets, live or frozen foods such as brine shrimp and bloodworms, and occasional vegetable matter.

Chapter 15: Gobies

Blue Neon Goby

The Blue Neon Goby has a sleek and elongated body, characterized by its vibrant blue coloration that ranges from deep turquoise to electric blue. The color extends over its body, including the dorsal, ventral, and anal fins.

Scientific Name: Stiphodon semoni
Care Level: Moderate
Temperament: Peaceful
Maximum Size: Up to 2.5 inches (6.5 cm)
Minimum Tank Size: 20 gallons
Water Conditions: 72-78°F (22-26°C); dKH 8-12; pH 7.5-8.5
Diet: Omnivorous, primarily feeds on algae and small invertebrates
Origin: Streams and rivers of Southeast Asia
Aquarium Type: Freshwater or brackish aquarium with ample hiding places

Notes:
Incorporate rocks, driftwood, and caves to provide hiding spots and replicate their natural habitat. Utilize live plants like Java Fern, Anubias, or aquatic mosses to enhance the aesthetics and create resting places. Use a fine-grain substrate like sand or smooth gravel to mimic the stream and riverbeds where Blue Neon Gobies are found. mploy gentle filtration to ensure water quality without creating strong currents, as Blue Neon Gobies prefer calmer waters. Opt for peaceful and non-aggressive tankmates that share similar water requirements. Avoid fin-nipping or larger fish that could intimidate the goby. Provide a balanced diet of high-quality pellets, algae-based foods, and occasional live or frozen small invertebrates. Ensure the diet includes algae to meet their nutritional needs.

16 Miscellaneous Fish

In this section, we introduce a variety of fish that are commonly found in many aquarium stores. These unique and intriguing species can be delightful additions to your aquarium.

Chapter 16: Miscellaneous Fish

Common Hatchet Fish

Hatchet fish typically exhibit a marbled appearance that blends shades of silver and black. Some might also possess a more uniform silver hue.

Scientific Name: Carnegiella strigata
Care Level: Moderate
Temperament: Peaceful
Maximum Size: 1.5" (4cm)
Minimum Tank Size: 20 Gallons (80 liters)
Water Conditions: 73-80° F, 22-26° C, dH 2-4, pH 6.5-7.0
Diet: Carnivore
Origin: Venezuela
Aquarium Type: Community

Notes:
Common Hatchet Fish are fond of floating plants and thrive best in schools of 5 or more. Their habitat should be enriched with driftwood, fine gravel, and an abundance of hiding spots and plant cover to mirror their natural surroundings. Given their propensity to jump, it's essential to ensure a snug-fitting tank lid. Common Hatchet Fish are surface dwellers, primarily staying near the water's surface. Thus, floating plants can help provide them with a feeling of security and a natural habitat. While they are generally peaceful, it's best to house them with species that won't nip at their fins. Their unique shape and slow-moving nature can make them a target for more aggressive or fin-nipping tankmates. While they might be initially hesitant to consume dried foods, they usually acclimatize to them with time. In addition to dried foods, their diet can be supplemented with frozen and live foods, including bloodworms and daphnia. If accessible, drosophila fruit flies make a nutritious treat.

Chapter 16: Miscellaneous Fish

Three-lined Pencil Fish

The Three-lined Pencil Fish is characterized by three distinct black horizontal stripes that span the entire length of its body.

Scientific Name: Nannostomus trifasciatus
Care Level: Moderate
Temperament: Peaceful
Maximum Size: 3" (7cm)
Minimum Tank Size: 30 Gallons (115 litre)
Water Conditions: 75-82° F, 23-27° C, dH 2-5, pH 6.5-7.0
Diet: Omnivore
Origin: South America
Aquarium Type: Community

Notes:
These fish thrive in environments with floating plants, replicating their natural habitat and providing them with a sense of security. eing schooling fish, they should be kept in groups of 5 or more, and they coexist best with fish of a similar size. ncorporate driftwood, fine gravel, and ample hiding spots with plant cover to make them feel at home. Despite their small mouth, they generally accept typical flake foods. However, to ensure a balanced diet, supplement with frozen and live foods like bloodworms and daphnia.

Chapter 16: Miscellaneous Fish

Butterfly Fish

Recognized by its distinct dark brown to black hue interspersed with lighter speckled colorations, the Butterfly Fish is more commonly referred to as the African Butterfly Fish.

Scientific Name: Pantodon buchholzi
Care Level: Moderate
Temperament: Aggressive
Maximum Size: 5" (12cm)
Minimum Tank Size: 30 Gallons (120 litre)
Water Conditions: 75-86° F, 23-30° C, dH 1-10, pH 6.9-7.1
Diet: Carnivore
Origin: Africa
Aquarium Type: Non-Community

Notes:
Naturally predatory, the Butterfly Fish predominantly remains near the water's surface, poised to ambush prey. When considering tank mates, ensure they are either of comparable aggression or size. The Butterfly Fish is likely to prey on any fish small enough to be swallowed. To replicate its natural habitat, arrange the tank with ample plants that extend close to the surface, offering the Butterfly Fish shelter and camouflage. Notably adept jumpers, these fish have been known to glide briefly through the air. It's essential to secure your tank with a tight-fitting lid. A varied diet consisting of small fish, brine shrimp, insects, and freeze-dried foods will keep them healthy and active.

Chapter 16: Miscellaneous Fish

Panchax Killifish

Characterized by its vivid blue/green or yellow hue, the Panchax Killifish features numerous red spots along its body.

Scientific Name: Aplocheilus lineatus
Care Level: Moderate
Temperament: Peaceful
Maximum Size: 2.5" (6cm)
Minimum Tank Size: 20 Gallons (80 litre)
Water Conditions: 75-86° F, 23-30° C, dH 1-10, pH 6.9-7.1
Diet: Carnivore
Origin: Sri Lanka
Aquarium Type: Community - primarily surface dwelling

Notes

Killifish come in various types, including the golden, clown, and gardneri variants. The term "Killi" originates from the Dutch word meaning "ditch" and does not suggest any aggressive behavior. When feeding, focus on live foods such as brine shrimp, white worms, and tubifex. They will also accept dry flake and frozen foods. Due to their preference for surface feeding, opt for foods that remain afloat. Panchax Killifish are generally peaceful but can be predatory towards smaller fish or invertebrates given their carnivorous diet. They can be paired well with mid or bottom-dwelling fish to create a dynamic and active aquarium environment. Given their preference for surface dwelling, floating plants can provide natural cover and encourage natural foraging behavior.

Chapter 16: Miscellaneous Fish

Parrot Cichlid

The Parrot Cichlid boasts vibrant hues that can range from bright red, orange, and yellow to muted grey. Ethically, it's crucial to steer clear of specimens that have undergone dye injections, a cruel practice which drastically reduces their lifespan.

Scientific Name: Hybrid Cichlid (it's important to note this fish is a man-made hybrid and doesn't have a specific scientific name)
Care Level: Intermediate
Temperament: Semi-aggressive
Maximum Size: 8" (20cm)
Minimum Tank Size: 55 Gallons (210 litre) (to provide adequate space for these sizable fish)
Water Conditions: 72-82° F (22-28° C), dH 1-10, pH 6.5-7.0
Diet: Omnivore
Origin: Man-made hybrid derived from South American cichlids
Aquarium Type: Community (but be cautious of tank mates due to their potential semi-aggressive behavior)

Notes

Parrot Cichlids are endearing aquatic pets with playful and quirky behaviors that entertain many aquarists. While they can be housed individually, they also thrive in small groups, provided the tank size is adequate. Their diet should encompass a variety of foods. While they do relish live foods like brine shrimp and worms, it's also essential to provide them with a balanced diet of high-quality flakes, pellets, and frozen foods. Due to their unique mouth shape, ensure that the food size is appropriate for easy consumption.

Index

A

Aggressive 11
Albino Corydoras 51
Albino Plec 58
Albino Sailfin Plec 58
Algae Eater 114
Altum Angelfish 123
Ammonia 15
anabantoids 88
Angelfish 123
Angels 122

B

Bala Shark 111
Banded Corydoras 35
Bandit Corydoras 44
Banjo Catfish 69
Bengal Loach 23
Betta Fish 99
Black Ghost Knifefish 143
Black Neon Tetra 72
Black Phantom Tetra 71
Black Ruby Barb 101
Blackstripe Bondi Corydoras 36
Bleeding Heart Tetra 73
Blood-fin Tetra 74
Blue Botia 24
Blue Corydoras 37
Blue Dolphin Cichlid 132
Blue Neon Goby 149
Blue Phantom Plec 60
Blue Ram 132
Boeseman's Rainbowfish 140

Index

Bondi Corydoras 36
Bristlenose Plecy 53
Bronze Corydoras 38
Buenos Aires Tetra 75
Bumblebee Cichlid 127, 131
Bumblebee Goby 147
Burmese Polkadot Loach 25
Butterfly Fish 153

C

Callichthyidae 34
Care Difficulty 11
Catfish 34
Chain Loach 27
Characidae 70
Characins 70
Checker Barb 102
Cherry Barb 103
Chocolate Gourami 89
Cichlidae 122, 134
Cichlids 122
Clown Barb 104
Clown Loach 26
Clown Plec 61
Cobitidae 22
Common Discus 135
Common Plec 54
Congo Tetra 76
Convict Cichlid 129
Cory Catfish 34
Cyprinidae 100, 116
Cyprinids 100

D

Danios 116
Discus 134
Dwarf Chain Loach 27
Dwarf Corydoras 39
Dwarf Gourami 90

E

Electric Fish 142
Elegant Corydoras 42

Index

Elephant Nose 145
Emerald Cory 41
Emperor Tetra 77
Endler's Livebearer 19

F

Featherfin Catfish 67
Fighting Fish 99
Flying Fox 105

G

Garra 64
GH 13
Ghost Knifefish 143
Giant Danio 117
Giant Gourami 91
Glowlight Danio 119
Glowlight Tetra 78
Gobies 146
Gobiidae 146
Golden Angelfish 125
Golden Barb 106
Golden Gourami 95
Golden Pristella Tetra 79
Gold Nugget Plec 55
Gourami 90, 93, 94, 95
Green Terror Cichlid 126
Guppy 18

H

Harlequin Rasbora 115
Hatchetfish 151
Hognosed Brochis 40
Horse-face Loach 28

I

Introduction 10

J

Jack Dempsey Cichlid 130
Julii Corydoras 43

K

Index

KH 13
Killifish 154
Kissing Gourami 97
Knifefish 143
Knight Goby 148
Koi Angelfish 124
Kribensis Cichlid 133
Kuhli Loach 29

L

Labyrinth Fish 88
Lemon Tetra 80
Leopard Sailfin Plec 56
Livebearers 16
Loaches 22
Loricariidae 52

M

Melanotaeniidae 138
Molly 20
Moonlight Gourami 97

N

Neo-electric fish 142
Neon Rainbowfish 141
Neon Tetra 81
Neotropical 142
Nitrate 15
Nitrite 15

O

Odessa Barb 107
One-spot Barb 107
Osphronemidae 88
Otocinclus Catfish 63

P

Panchax 154
Panda Corydoras 45
Panda Garra 64
Paradise Fish 92
Parrot Cichlid 155
Peaceful 11
Pearl Danio 118

Index

Pearl Gourami 93
Pencilfish 152
Penguin Tetra 82
Peppered Corydoras 46
pH 13
Phantom Tetra 71
Pictus Catfish 65
Platy 17
Plecos 52
Poeciliidae 16
Polkadot Loach 25
Pygmy Sparkling Gourami 96

R

Rainbow Fish 138
Rainbow Shark 113
Rams 128
Rasbora 115
Red Checkerboard Discus 137
Red Discus 136
Red-eye Tetra 83
Red Line Torpedo Barb 108
Red Phantom Tetra 84
Red Rainbowfish 139
Red-Tailed Black Shark 112
Royal Plec 59
Royal Red Discus 136
Ruby Rainbow Shark 113
Rummy Nose Tetra 85

S

Sailfin Plec 56, 58
Salt & Pepper Corydoras 47
Schwartz's Catfish 48
Semi-Aggressive 11
Serpae Tetra 86
Shark 111, 112, 113
Siamese Algae Eater 114
Siamese Fighting Fish 98
Silver Dollar 87
Silver/Moonlight Gourami 97
Skunk Loach 30
Sterba's Corydoras 50
Striped Raphael 68
Sword Tail 21

Index

T

Temperament 11
Temperature 12
Three Spot Gourami 94
Tiger Barb 109
Tinfoil Barb 110
Torpedo Barb 108

W

Water Hardness 13
Water Parameters 12
Weather Loach 33
Whiptail Catfish 66

Y

Yoyo Loach 31

Z

Zebra Danio 120
Zebra Knifefish 144
Zebra Loach 32
Zebra Plec 57

SOMETHING NOT COVERED?

We want to create the best possible resources to help you learn and get things done, so if we've missed anything out, then please get in touch using the links below and let us know. Thanks.

 office@elluminetpress.com

 elluminetpress.com/feedback

www.ingramcontent.com/pod-product-compliance
Lightning Source LLC
Chambersburg PA
CBHW050235120526
44590CB00016B/2098